*Also by Stephen King and available
from New English Library*

NIGHTSHIFT
'SALEM'S LOT
THE SHINING
THE STAND

CARRIE
Stephen King

NEW ENGLISH LIBRARY

First published in Great Britain by
New English Library Ltd., 1974

First NEL Open Market Edition 1975
New edition July 1975
New edition April 1978
Reprinted November 1978
Reprinted June 1979
Reprinted October 1979
Reprinted February 1981
New edition April 1981
Reprinted December 1981
Reprinted August 1982

NEL Books are published by
New English Library,
Mill Road, Dunton Green,
Sevenoaks, Kent,
a division of Hodder and Stoughton Ltd.

Printed and bound in Great Britain by
©ollins, Glasgow

0 450 05475 6

This is for Tabby, who got me into it —
and then bailed me out of it

The lines on page 38 are from *Just Like a Woman*.
The lines on page 220 are from *Tombstone Blues*.
Both songs were written by Bob Dylan.

Part One

Blood Sport

News item from the Westover (Me.) weekly *Enterprise*, August 19, 1966:

RAIN OF STONES REPORTED

It was reliably reported by several persons that a rain of stones fell from a clear blue sky on Carlin Street in the town of Chamberlain on August 17th. The stones fell principally on the home of Mrs Margaret White, damaging the roof extensively and ruining two gutters and a downspout valued at approximately $25. Mrs White, a widow, lives with her three-year-old daughter, Carietta.

Mrs White could not be reached for comment.

Nobody was really surprised when it happened, not really, not at the subconscious level where savage things grow. On the surface, all the girls in the shower room were shocked, thrilled, ashamed, or simply glad that the White bitch had taken it in the mouth again. Some of them might also have claimed surprise, but of course their claim was untrue. Carrie had been going to school with some of them since the first grade, and this had been building since that time, building slowly and immutably, in accordance with all the laws that govern human nature, building with all the steadiness of a chain reaction approaching critical mass.

What none of them knew, of course, was that Carrie White was telekinetic.

Graffiti scratched on a desk of the Barker Street

Grammar school in Chamberlain:
Carrie White eats shit.

The locker room was filled with shouts, echoes, and the subterranean sound of showers splashing on tile. The girls had been playing volleyball in Period One, and their morning sweat was light and eager.

Girls stretched and writhed under the hot water, squalling, flicking water, squirting white bars of soap from hand to hand. Carrie stood among them stolidly, a frog among swans. She was a chunky girl with pimples on her neck and back and buttocks, her wet hair completely without colour. It rested against her face with dispirited sogginess and she simply stood, head slightly bent, letting the water splat against her flesh and roll off. She looked the part of the sacrificial goat, the constant butt, believer in left-handed monkey wrenches, perpetual foul-up, and she was. She wished forlornly and constantly that Ewen High had individual—and thus private—showers, like the high schools at Andover or Boxford. They stared. They always *stared*.

Showers turning off one by one, girls stepping out, removing pastel bathing caps, towelling, spraying deodorant, checking the clock over the door. Bras were hooked, underpants stepped into. Steam hung in the air; the place might have been an Egyptian bathhouse except for the constant rumble of the Jacuzzi whirlpool bath in the corner. Calls and catcalls rebounded with all the snap and flicker of billiard balls after a hard break.

'—so Tommy said he *hated* it on me and I—'

'—I'm going with my sister and her husband. He picks his nose but so does she, so they're very—'

'—shower after school and—'

'—too cheap to spend a goddam penny so Cindi and I—'

Miss Desjardin, their slim, nonbreasted gym teacher, stepped in, craned her neck around briefly, and slapped her hands together once, smartly. 'What are you waiting for, Carrie? Doom? Bell in five minutes.' Her shorts were blinding white, her legs not too curved but striking in their unobtrusive muscularity. A silver whistle, won in college archery competition, hung around her neck.

The girls giggled and Carrie looked up, her eyes slow and dazed from the heat and the steady, pounding roar of the water. 'Ohuh?'

It was a strangely froggy sound, grotesquely apt, and the girls giggled again. Sue Snell had whipped a towel from her hair with the speed of a magician embarking on a wondrous feat and began to comb rapidly. Miss Desjardin made an irritated cranking gesture at Carrie and stepped out.

Carrie turned off the shower. It died in a drip and a gurgle.

It wasn't until she stepped out that they all saw the blood running down her leg.

From The Shadow Exploded: Documented Facts and Specific Conclusions Derived from the Case of Carietta White, by David R. Congress (Tulane University Press: 1981), p. 34:

It can hardly be disputed that failure to note specific instances of telekinesis during the White girl's earlier years must be attributed to the conclusions offered by White and Stearns in their paper *Telekinesis: A Wild Talent Revisited*—that the ability to move objects by effort of the will alone comes to the fore only in moments of extreme personal stress. The talent is well hidden indeed; how else could it have remained submerged for centuries with only the tip of the iceberg showing above a sea of quackery?

We have only skimpy hearsay evidence upon which to lay our foundation in this case, but even this is enough to indicate that a 'TK' potential of immense magnitude existed within Carrie White. The great tragedy is that we are now all Monday-morning quarterbacks . . .

'*Per*-iod!'

The catcall came first from Chris Hargensen. It struck the tiled walls, rebounded, and struck again. Sue Snell gasped laughter from her nose and felt an odd, vexing mixture of hate, revulsion, exasperation, and pity. She just looked so *dumb,* standing there, not knowing what was going on. God, you'd think she never—

'*PER*-iod!'

It was becoming a chant, an incantation. Someone in the back-ground (perhaps Hargensen again, Sue couldn't tell in the jungle of echoes) was yelling *'Plug it up!'* with hoarse, uninhibited abandon.

'*PER*-iod, *PER*-iod, *PER*-iod!'

Carrie stood dumbly in the centre of a forming circle, water rolling from her skin in beads. She stood like a patient ox, aware that the joke was on her (as always), dumbly embarrassed but unsurprised.

Sue felt welling disgust as the first dark drops of menstrual blood struck the tile in dime-sized drops. 'For God's sake Carrie, you got your period!' Sue cried. 'Clean yourself up!'

'Ohuh?'

She looked around bovinely. Her hair stuck to her cheeks in a curving helmet shape. There was a cluster of acne on one shoulder. At sixteen, the elusive stamp of hurt was already marked clearly in her eyes.

'She thinks they're for lipstick!' Ruth Grogan suddenly shouted with cryptic glee, and then burst into a shriek of laughter. Sue remembered the comment later and fitted it into a general picture, but now it was only another senseless sound in the confusion. *Sixteen?* She was thinking. *She must know what's happening, she—*

More droplets of blood. Carrie still blinked around at her classmates in slow bewilderment.

Helen Shyres turned around and made mock throwing-up gestures.

'You're *bleeding*!' Sue yelled suddenly, furiously. 'You're *bleeding*, you big dumb pudding!'

Carrie looked down at herself.

She shrieked.

The sound was very loud in the humid locker room.

A tampon suddenly struck her in the chest and fell with a plop at her feet. A red flower stained the absorbent cotton and spread.

Then the laughter, disgusted, contemptuous, horrified, seemed to rise and bloom into something jagged and ugly, and the girls were bombarding her with tampons and sanitary napkins, some from purses, some from the broken dispenser on the wall. They flew like snow and the chant became: 'Plug it *up*. plug it *up*. plug it—'

Sue was throwing them too, throwing and chanting with the rest, not really sure what she was doing—a charm had occurred to her mind and it glowed there like neon: *There's no harm in it really no harm in it really no harm—*It was still flashing and glowing, reassuringly, when Carrie suddenly began to howl and back away, flailing her arms and grunting and gobbling.

The girls stopped, realizing that fission and explosion had finally been reached. It was at this point, when looking back, that some of them would claim surprise. Yet there had been all these years, all these years of let's short-sheet Carrie's bed at Christian Youth Camp and I found this love letter from Carrie to Flash Bobby Pickett let's copy it and pass it around and hide her underpants

13

somewhere and put this snake in her shoe and duck her *again*, duck her *again*: Carrie tagging along stubbornly on biking trips, known one year as pudd'n and the next year as truck-face, always smelling sweaty, not able to catch up; catching poison ivy from urinating in the bushes and everyone finding out (hey, scratch-ass, your bum itch?). Billy Preston putting peanut butter in her hair that time she fell asleep in study hall; the pinches, the legs outstretched in school aisles to trip her up, the books knocked from her desk, the obscene postcard tucked into her purse; Carrie on the church picnic and kneeling down clumsily to pray and the seam of her old madras skirt splitting along the zipper like the sound of a huge wind-breakage; Carrie always missing the ball, even in kick-ball, falling on her face in Modern Dancing during their sophomore year and chipping a tooth, running into the net during volleyball; wearing stockings that were always run, running, or about to run, always showing sweat stains under the arms of her blouses; even the time Chris Hargensen called up after school from the Kelly Fruit Company downtown and asked her if she knew that *pig poop* was spelled C-A-R-R-I-E: Suddenly all this and the critical mass was reached. The ultimate shit-on, gross-out, put-down, long searched for, was found. Fission.

She backed away, howling in the new silence, fat forearms crossing her face, a tampon stuck in the middle of her pubic hair.

The girls watched her, their eyes shining solemnly.

Carrie backed into the side of one of the four large shower compartments and slowly collapsed into a sitting position. Slow, helpless groans jerked out of her. Her eyes rolled with wet whiteness, like the eyes of a hog in the slaughtering pen.

Sue said slowly, hesitantly: 'I think this must be the first time she ever—'

That was when the door pumped open with a flat and hurried bang and Miss Desjardin burst in to see what the matter was.

From *The Shadow Exploded* (p. 41):

Both medical and psychological writers on the subject are in agreement that Carrie White's exceptionally late and traumatic commencement of the menstrual cycle might well have provided the trigger for her latent talent.

It seems incredible that, as late as 1979, Carrie knew nothing of the mature woman's monthly cycle. It is nearly as incredible to believe that the girl's mother would permit her daughter to reach the age of nearly seventeen without consulting a gynaecologist concerning the daughter's failure to menstruate.

Yet the facts are incontrovertible. When Carrie White realized she was bleeding from the vaginal opening, she had no idea of what was taking place. She was innocent of the entire concept of menstruation.

One of her surviving classmates, Ruth Gogan, tells of entering the girls' locker room at Ewen High School the year before the events we are concerned with and seeing Carrie using a tampon to blot her lipstick with. At that time Miss Gogan said: 'What the hell are you up to?' Miss White replied: 'Isn't this right?' Miss Gogan then replied: 'Sure. Sure it is.' Ruth Gogan let a number of her girl friends in on this (she later told this interviewer she thought it was 'sorta cute'), and if anyone tried in the future to inform Carrie of the true purpose of what she was using to make up with, she apparently dismissed the explanation as an attempt to pull her leg. This was a facet of her life that she had become exceedingly wary of . . .

When the girls were gone to their Period Two classes and

15

the bell had been silenced (several of them had slipped quietly out the back door before Miss Desjardin could begin to take names), Miss Desjardin employed the standard tactic for hysterics: She slapped Carrie smartly across the face. She hardly would have admitted the pleasure the act gave her, and she certainly would have denied that she regarded Carrie as a fat, whiny bag of lard. A first-year teacher, she still believed that she thought all children were good.

Carrie looked up at her dumbly, face still contorted and working. 'M-M-Miss D-D-Des-D—'

'Get up,' Miss Desjardin said dispassionately. 'Get up and tend to yourself.'

'I'm bleeding to death!' Carrie screamed, and one blind, searching hand came up and clutched Miss Desjardin's white shorts. It left a bloody handprint.

'I . . . you . . .' The gym teacher's face contorted into a pucker of disgust, and she suddenly hurled Carrie, stumbling, to her feet *'Get over there!'*

Carrie stood swaying between the showers and the wall with its dime sanitary-napkin dispenser, slumped over, breasts pointing at the floor, her arms dangling limply. She looked like an ape. Her eyes were shiny and blank.

'Now,' Miss Desjardin said with hissing, deadly emphasis, 'you take one of those napkins out . . . no, never mind the coin slot, it's broken anyway . . . take one and . . . damn it, will you *do* it! You act as if you never had a period before.'

'Period?' Carrie said.

Her expression of complete unbelief was too genuine, too full of dumb and hopeless horror, to be ignored or denied. A terrible and black foreknowledge grew in Rita Desjardin's mind. It was incredible, could not be. She herself had begun menstruation shortly after her eleventh birthday and had gone to the head of the stairs to yell

16

down excitedly: 'Hey, Mum, I'm on the rag!'

'Carrie?' she said now. She advanced toward the girl. 'Carrie?'

Carrie flinched away. At the same instant, a rack of softball bats in the corner fell over with a large, echoing bang. They rolled every which way, making Desjardin jump.

'Carrie, is this your first period?'

But now that the thought had been admitted, she hardly had to ask. The blood was dark and flowing with terrible heaviness. Both of Carrie's legs were smeared and splattered with it, as though she had waded through a river of blood.

'It hurts,' Carrie groaned. 'My stomach . . .'

'That passes,' Miss Desjardin said. Pity and self-shame met in her and mixed uneasily. 'You have to . . . uh, stop the flow of blood. You—'

There was a bright flash overhead, followed by a flashgunlike pop as a lightbulb sizzled and went out. Miss Desjardin cried out with surprise, and it occurred to her (the whole damn place is falling in) that this kind of thing always seemed to happen around Carrie when she was upset, as if bad luck dogged her every step. The thought was gone almost as quickly as it had come. She took one of the sanitary napkins from the broken dispenser and unwrapped it.

'Look,' she said, 'Like this—'

From *The Shadow Exploded* (p. 54):

Carrie White's mother, Margaret White, gave birth to her daughter on September 21, 1963, under circumstances which can only be termed bizarre. In fact, an overview of the Carrie White case leaves the careful student with one feeling ascendant over all others: that Carrie was the only issue of a family as odd as any that has ever been brought to popular attention.

As noted earlier, Ralph White died in February of 1963 when a steel girder fell out of a carrying sling on a housing-project job in Portland. Mrs White continued to live alone in their suburban Chamberlain bungalow.

Due to the White's near-fanatical fundamentalist religious beliefs, Mrs White had no friends to see her through her period of bereavement. And when her labour began seven months later, she was alone.

At approximately 1:30 P.M. on September 21, the neighbours on Carlin Street began to hear screams from the White bungalow. The police, however, were not summoned to the scene until after 6:00 P.M. We are left with two unappetizing alternatives to explain this time lag: Either Mrs White's neighbours on the street did not wish to become involved in a police·investigation, or dislike for her had become so strong that they deliberately adopted a wait-and-see attitude. Mrs Georgia McLaughlin, the only one of the three remaining residents who were on the street at that time and who would talk to me, said that she did not call the police because she thought the screams had something to do with 'holy rollin'.'

When the police did arrive at 6:22 P.M. the screams had become irregular. Mrs White was found in her bed upstairs, and the investigating officer, Thomas G. Mearton, at first thought she had been the victim of an assault. The bed was drenched with blood, and a butcher knife lay on the floor. It was only then that he saw the baby, still partially wrapped in the placental membrane, at Mrs White's breast. She had apparently cut the umbilical cord herself with the knife.

It staggers both imagination and belief to advance the hypothesis that Mrs Margaret White did not know she was pregnant, or even understand what the word entails, and recent scholars such as J. W. Bankson and George Felding have made a more reasonable case for the hypothesis that the concept, linked irrevocably in her mind with the 'sin' of intercourse, had been blocked entirely from her mind. She may simply have refused to believe that such a thing could happen to her.

We have records of at least three letters to a friend in Kenosha, Wisconsin, that seem to prove conclusively that Mrs White believed, from her fifth month on, that she had 'a cancer of the womanly parts' and would soon join her husband in heaven . . .

When Miss Desjardin led Carrie up to the office fifteen minutes later, the halls were mercifully empty. Classes droned onwards behind closed doors.

Carrie's shrieks had finally ended, but she had continued to weep with steady regularity. Desjardin had finally placed the napkin herself, cleaned the girl up with wet paper towels, and gotten her back into her plain cotton underpants.

She tried twice to explain the commonplace reality of menstruation, but Carrie clapped her hands over her ears and continued to cry.

Mr Morton, the assistant principal, was out of his office in a flash when they entered. Billy deLois and Henry Trennant, two boys waiting for the lecture due them for cutting French I, goggled around from their chairs.

'Come in,' Mr Morton said briskly. 'Come right in.' He glared over Desjardin's shoulder at the boys, who were staring at the bloody handprint on her shorts. 'What are *you* looking at?'

'Blood,' Henry said, and smiled with a kind of vacuous surprise.

'Two detention periods,' Morton snapped. He glanced

down at the bloody handprint and blinked.

He closed the door behind them and began pawing through the top drawer of his filing cabinet for a school accident form.

'Are you all right, uh—?'

'Carrie,' Desjardin supplied. 'Carrie White.' Mr Morton had finally located an accident form. There was a large coffee stain on it. 'You won't need that, Mr Morton.'

'I suppose it was the trampoline. We just . . . I won't?'

'No. But I think Carrie should be allowed to go home for the rest of the day. She's had a rather frightening experience.' Her eyes flashed a signal which he caught but could not interpret.

'Yes, okay, if you say so. Good. Fine.' Morton crumpled the form back into the filing cabinet, slammed it shut with his thumb in the drawer, and grunted. He whirled gracefully to the door, yanked it open, glared at Billy and Henry, and called: 'Miss Fish, could we have a dismissal slip here, please? Carrie Wright.'

'White,' said Miss Desjardin.

'White,' Morton agreed.

Billy deLois sniggered.

'Week's detention!' Morton barked. A blood blister was forming under his thumbnail. Hurt like hell. Carrie's steady, monotonous weeping went on and on.

Miss Fish brought the yellow dismissal slip and Morton scrawled his initials on it with his silver pocket pencil, wincing at the pressure on his wounded thumb.

'Do you need a ride, Cassie?' he asked. 'We can call a cab if you need one.'

She shook her head. He noticed with distaste that a large bubble of green mucus had formed at one nostril. Morton looked over her head and at Miss Desjardin.

'I'm sure she'll be all right,' she said. 'Carrie only has to go over to Carlin Street. The fresh air will do her good.'

Morton gave the girl the yellow slip. 'You can go now, Cassie,' he said magnanimously.

'That's not my name!' she screamed suddenly.

Morton recoiled, and Miss Desjardin jumped as if struck from behind. The heavy ceramic ashtray on Morton's desk (it was Rodin's *Thinker* with his head turned into a receptacle for cigarette butts) suddenly toppled to the rug, as if to take cover from the force of her scream. Butts and flakes of Morton's pipe tobacco scattered on the pale-green nylon rug.

'Now, listen,' Morton said, trying to muster sternness, 'I know you're upset, but that doesn't mean I'll stand for—'

'Please,' Miss Desjardin said quietly.

Morton blinked at her and then nodded curtly. He tried to project the image of a lovable John Wayne figure while performing the disciplinary functions that were his main job as Assistant Principal, but did not succeed very well. The administration (usually represented at Jay Cee suppers, P.T.A. functions, and American Legion award ceremonies by Principal Henry Grayle) usually termed him 'lovable Mort.' The student body was more apt to term him 'that crazy ass-jabber from the office.' But, as few students such as Billy deLois and Henry Trennant spoke at P.T.A. functions or town meetings, the administration's view tended to carry the day.

Now lovable Mort, still secretly nursing his jammed thumb, smiled at Carrie and said, 'Go along then if you like, Miss Wright. Or would you like to sit a spell and just collect yourself?'

'I'll go,' she muttered, and swiped at her hair. She got up, then looked around at Miss Desjardin. Her eyes were wide open and dark with knowledge. 'They laughed at me. Threw things. They've *always* laughed.'

21

Desjardin could only look at her helplessly.

Carrie left.

For a moment there was silence; Morton and Desjardin watched her go. Then, with an awkward throat-clearing sound, Mr Morton hunkered down carefully and began to sweep together the debris from the fallen ashtray.

'What was *that* all about?'

She sighed and looked at the drying maroon hand-print on her shorts with distaste. 'She got her period. Her first period. In the shower.'

Morton cleared his throat again and his cheeks went pink. The sheet of paper he was sweeping with moved even faster. 'Isn't she a bit, uh—'

'Old for her first? Yes. That's what made it so traumatic for her. Although I can't understand why her mother . . .' The thought trailed off, forgotten for the moment. 'I don't think I handled it very well, Morty, but I didn't understand what was going on. She thought she was bleeding to death.'

He stared up sharply.

'I don't believe she knew there was such a thing as menstruation until half an hour ago.'

'Hand me that little brush there, Miss Desjardin. Yes, that's it.' She handed him a little brush with the legend *Chamberlain Hardware and Lumber Company NEVER Brushes You Off* written up the handle. He began to brush his pile of ashes on to the paper. 'There's still going to be some for the vacuum cleaner, I guess. This deep pile is miserable. I thought I set that ashtray back on the desk further. Funny how things fall over.' He bumped his head on the desk and sat up abruptly. 'It's hard for me to believe that a girl in this or any other high school could get through three years and still be alien to the fact of menstruation, Miss Desjardin.'

'It's even more difficult for me,' she said. 'But it's all I can think of to explain her reaction. And she's always been a group scapegoat.'

'Um.' He funnelled the ashes and butts into the wastebasket and dusted his hands. 'I've placed her, I think. White. Margaret White's daughter. Must be. That makes it a little easier to believe.' He sat down behind his desk and smiled apologetically. 'There's so many of them. After five years or so, they all start to merge into one group face. You call boys by their brother's names, that type of thing. It's hard.'

'Of course it is.'

'Wait 'til you've been in the game twenty years, like me,' he said morosely, looking down at his blood blister. 'You get kids that look familiar and find out you had their daddy the year you started teaching. Margaret White was before my time, for which I am profoundly grateful. She told Mrs Bicente, God rest her, that the Lord was reserving a special burning seat in hell for her because she gave the kids an outline of Mr Darwin's beliefs on evolution. She was suspended twice while she was here— once for beating a classmate with her purse. Legend has it that Margaret saw the classmate smoking a cigarette. Peculiar religious views. Very peculiar.' His John Wayne expression suddenly snapped down. 'The other girls. Did they really laugh at her?'

'Worse. They were yelling and throwing sanitary napkins at her when I walked in. Throwing them like . . . like peanuts.'

'Oh. Oh, dear.' John Wayne disappeared. Mr Morton went scarlet. 'You have names?'

'Yes. Not all of them, although some of them may rat on the rest. Christine Hargensen appeared to be the ringleader . . . as usual.'

'Chris and her Mortimer Snurds,' Morton murmured.

'Yes. Tina Blake, Rachel Spies, Helen Shyres, Donna

23

Thibodeau and her sister Fern, Lila Grace, Jessica Upshaw. And Sue Snell.' She frowned. 'You wouldn't expect a trick like that from Sue. She's never seemed the type for this kind of a—stunt.'

'Did you talk to the girls involved?'

Miss Desjardin chuckled unhappily. 'I got them the hell out of there. I was too flustered. And Carrie was having hysterics.'

'Um.' He steepled his fingers. 'Do you plan to talk to them?'

'Yes.' But she sounded reluctant.

'Do I detect a note of—'

'You probably do,' she said glumly. 'I'm living in a glass house, see. I understand how those girls felt. The whole thing just made me want to take the girl and *shake* her. Maybe there's some kind of instinct about menstruation that makes women want to snarl, I don't know. I keep seeing Sue Snell and the way she looked.'

'Um,' Mr Morton repeated wisely. He did not understand women and had no urge at all to discuss menstruation.

'I'll talk to them tomorrow,' she promised, rising. 'Rip them down one side and up the other.'

'Good. Make the punishment suit the crime. And if you feel you have to send any of them to, ah, to me, feel free—'

'I will,' she said kindly. 'By the way, a light blew out while I was trying to calm her down. It added the final touch.'

'I'll send a janitor right down,' he promised. 'And thanks for doing your best, Miss Desjardin. Will you have Miss Fish send in Billy and Henry?'

'Certainly.' She left.

He leaned back and let the whole business slide out of his mind. When Billy deLois and Henry Trennant, class-cutters *extraordinaire,* slunk in, he glared at them happily

24

and prepared to talk tough.

As he often told Hank Grayle, he ate class-cutters for lunch.

Graffiti scratched on a desk in Chamberlain Junior High School:

Roses are red, violets are blue, sugar is sweet, but Carrie White eats shit.

She walked down Ewin Avenue and crosssed over to Carlin at the stoplight on the corner. Her head was down and she was trying to think of nothing. Cramps came and went in great, gripping waves, making her slow down and speed up like a car with carburettor trouble. She stared at the sidewalk. Quartz glittering in the cement. Hop-scotch grids scratched in ghostly, rain-faded chalk. Wads of gum stamped flat. Pieces of tinfoil and penny-candy wrappers. *They all hate and they never stop. They never get tired of it.* A penny lodged in a crack. She kicked it. *Imagine Chris Hargensen all bloody and screaming for mercy. With rats crawling all over her face. Good. Good. That would be good.* A dog turd with a foot-track in the middle of it. A roll of blackened caps that some kid had banged with a stone. Cigarette butts. *Crash in her head with a rock, with a boulder. Crash in all their hearts. Good. Good.*

(saviour jesus meek and mild)

That was good for Momma, all right for her. She didn't have to go among the wolves every day of every year, out into a carnival of laughers, joke-tellers, pointers, snickerers. And didn't Momma say there would be a Day of Judgment.

(the name of that star shall be wormwood and they shall be scourged with scorpions)

and an angel with a sword?

If only it would be today and Jesus coming not with a

25

lamb and a shepherd's crook, but with a boulder on each hand to crush the laughters and the snickerers, to root out the evil and destroy it screaming—a terrible Jesus of blood and righteousness.

And if only she could be His sword and His arm.

She had tried to fit. She had defied Momma in a hundred little ways, had tried to erase the red-plague circle that had been drawn around her from the first day she had left the controlled environment of the small house on Carlin Street and had walked up to the Baker Street Grammar School with her Bible under her arm. She could still remember that day, the stares, and the sudden, awful silence when she had gotten down on her knees before lunch in the school cafeteria—the laughter had begun on that day and had echoed up through the years.

The red-plague circle was like blood itself—you could scrub and scrub and scrub and still it would be there, not erased, not clean. She had never gotten on her knees in a public place again, although she had not told Momma that. Still, the original memory remained, with her and with *them*. She had fought Momma tooth and nail over the Christian Church Camp, and had earned the money to go herself by taking in sewing. Momma told her darkly that it was Sin, that it was Methodists and Baptists and Congregationalists and that it was Sin and Backsliding. She forbade Carrie to swim at the camp. Yet although she *had* swum and *had* laughed when they ducked her (until she couldn't get her breath any more and they kept doing it and she got panicky and began to scream) and had tried to take part in the camp's activities, a thousand practical jokes had been played on ol' prayin' Carrie and she had come home on the bus a week early, her eyes red and socketed from weeping, to be picked up by Momma at the station, and Momma had told her grimly that she should treasure the memory of her scourging as proof that

26

Momma knew, that Momma was right, that the only hope of safety and salvation was inside the red circle. 'For straight is the gate,' Momma said grimly in the taxi, and at home she had sent Carrie to the closet for six hours.

Momma had, of course, forbade her to shower with the other girls; Carrie had hidden her shower things in her school locker and had showered anyway, taking part in a naked ritual that was shameful and embarrassing to her in hopes that the circle around her might fade a little, just a little—

(but today o today)

Tommy Erbter, age five, was biking up the other side of the street. He was a small, intense-looking boy on a twenty-inch Schwinn with bright-red training wheels. He was humming 'Scoobie Doo, where are you?' under his breath. He saw Carrie, brightened, and stuck out his tongue.

'Hey, ol' fart-face! Ol' prayin' Carrie!'

Carrie glared at him with sudden smoking rage. The bike wobbled on its training wheels and suddenly fell over. Tommy screamed. The bike was on top of him. Carrie smiled and walked on. The sound of Tommy's wails was sweet, jangling music in her ears.

If only she could make something like that happen whenever she liked.

(just did)

She stopped dead seven houses up from her own, staring blankly at nothing. Behind her, Tommy was climbing tearfully back on to his bike, nursing a scraped knee. He yelled something at her, but she ignored it. She had been yelled at by experts.

She had been thinking:

(fall off that bike kid push you off that bike and split your rotten head)

And something had *happened*

27

Her mind had . . . had . . . she groped for a word. Had
flexed. That was not just right, but it was very close. There
had been a curious mental bending, almost like an elbow
curling a dumbbell. That wasn't exactly right either, but it
was all she could think of. An elbow with no strength. A
weak baby muscle.

Flex.

She suddenly stared fiercely at Mrs Yorraty's big
picture window. She thought:

(stupid frumpty old bitch break that window)

Nothing. Mrs Yorraty's picture window glittered
serenely in the fresh nine o'clock glow of morning.
Another cramp gripped Carrie's belly and she walked on.

But . . .

The light. And the ashtray; don't forget the ashtray.

She looked back

(old bitch hates my momma)

over her shoulder. Again it seemed that something
flexed . . . but very weakly. The flow of her thoughts
shuddered as if there had been a sudden bubbling from a
wellspring deeper inside.

The picture window seemed to ripple. Nothing more. It
could have been her eyes. *Could* have been.

Her head began to feel tired and fuzzy, and it throbbed
with the beginning of a headache. Her eyes were hot, as if
she had just sat down and read the Book of Revelations
straight through.

She continued to walk down the street toward the small
white house with the blue shutters. The familiar hate-
love-dread feeling was churning inside her. Ivy had
crawled up the west side of the bungalow (they always
called it the bungalow because the White house sounded
like a political joke and Momma said all politicians were
crooks and sinners and would eventually give the country
over to the Godless Reds who would put all the believers

of Jesus—even the Catholics—up against the wall), and the ivy was picturesque, she *knew* it was, but sometimes she hated it. Sometimes, like now, the ivy looked like a grotesque giant hand ridged with great veins which had sprung up out of the ground to grip the building. She approached it with dragging feet.

Of course, there had been the stones.

She stopped again, blinking vapidly at the day. The stones. Momma never talked about that; Carrie didn't even know if her momma still remembered the day of the stones. It was surprising that she herself still remembered it. She had been a very little girl then. How old? Three? Four? There had been the girl in the white bathing suit, and then the stones came. And things had flown in the house. Here the memory was, suddenly bright and clear. As if it had been here all along, just below the surface, waiting for a kind of mental puberty.

Waiting, maybe, for today.

From *Carrie: The Black Dawn of T. K. (Esquire* Magazine, September 12, 1980) by Jack Gaver:

Estelle Horan had lived in the neat San Diego suburb of Parrish for twelve years, and outwardly she is typical Mrs California: She wears bright print shifts and smoked amber sunglasses; her hair is black-streaked blonde; she drives a neat maroon Volkswagen Formula Vee with a smile decal on the petrol cap and a green-flag ecology sticker on the back window. Her husband is an executive at the Parrish branch of the Bank of America; her son and daughter are certified members of the Southern California Sun 'n Fun Crowd, burnished-brown beach creatures. There is a hibachi in the small, beautifully kept back yard, and the door chimes play a tinkly phrase from the refrain of 'Hey, Jude.'

But Mrs Horan still carries the thin, difficult soil of New England somewhere inside her, and when she talks of Carrie White her face takes on an odd, pinched look that is more like Lovecraft out of Arkham than Kerouac out of Southern Cal.

'Of course she was strange,' Estelle Horan tells me, lighting a second Virginia Slim a moment after stubbing out her first. 'The whole family was strange. Ralph was a construction worker, and people on the street said he carried a Bible and a .38 revolver to work with him every day. The Bible was for his coffee break and lunch. The .38 was in case he met Antichrist on the job. I can remember the Bible myself. The revolver . . . who knows? He was a big olive-skinned man with his hair always shaved into a flattop crewcut. He always looked mean. And you didn't meet his eyes, not ever. They were so intense they actually seemed to glow. When you saw him coming you crossed the street and you never stuck out your tongue at his back, not ever. That's how spooky *he* was.'

She pauses, puffing clouds of cigarette smoke toward the pseudo-redwood beams that cross the ceiling. Stella Horan lived on Carlin Street until she was twenty, commuting to day classes at Lewin Business College in Motton. But she remembers the incidents of the stones very clearly.

'There are times,' she says, 'when I wonder if I might have caused it. Their back yard was next to ours, and Mrs White had put in a hedge but it hadn't grown out yet. She'd called my mother dozens of times about "the show" I was putting on in my back yard. Well, my bathing suit was perfectly decent—prudish by today's standards— nothing but a plain old one-piece Jantzen. Mrs White used to go on and on about what a scandal it was for "her baby." My mother . . . well, she tries to be polite, but her temper is *so* quick. I don't know what Margaret White said to finally push her over the edge—called me the Whore of Babylon, I suppose—but my mother told her our yard was our yard and I'd go out and dance the hootchie-kootchie buck naked if that was her pleasure and mine. She also told her that she was a dirty old woman with a can of worms for a mind. There was a lot more shouting, but that was the upshot of it.

'I wanted to stop sunbathing right then. I hate trouble. It upsets my stomach. But Mom—when she gets a case, she's a terror. She came home from Jordan Marsh with a little white bikini. Told me I might as well get all the sun I could. "After all," she said, "the privacy of our own back yard and all." '

Stella Horan smiles a little at the memory and crushes out her cigarette.

'I tried to argue with her, tell her I didn't want any more trouble, didn't want to be a pawn in their back-fence war. Didn't do a bit of good. Trying to stop my mum when she gets a bee in her hat is like trying to stop a Mack truck going downhill with no brakes. Actually, there was more to it. I was scared of the Whites. Real religious nuts are nothing to fool with. Sure, Ralph White was dead, but what if Margaret still had that .38 around?

'But there I was on Saturday afternoon, spread out on a blanket in the back yard, covered with suntan lotion and listening to Top Forty on the radio. Mom hated that stuff and usually she'd yell out at least twice for me to turn it down before she went nuts. But that day she turned it up twice herself. I started to feel like the Whore of Babylon myself.

'But nobody came out of the Whites' place. Not even the old lady to hang her wash. That's something else—she never hung any undies on the back line. Not even Carrie's, and she was only three back then. Always in the house.

31

'I started to relax. I guess I was thinking Margaret must have taken Carrie to the park to worship God in the raw or something. Anyway, after a little while I rolled on my back, put one arm over my eyes, and dozed off.

'When I woke up, Carrie was standing next to me and looking down at my body.'

She breaks off, frowning into space. Outside, the cars are whizzzing by endlessly. I can hear the steady little whine my tape recorder makes. But it all seems a little too brittle, too glossy, just a cheap patina over a darker world—a real world where nightmares happen.

'She was such a *pretty* girl,' Stella Horan resumes, lighting another cigarette. 'I've seen some high school pictures of her, and that horrible fuzzy black-and-white photo on the cover of *Newsweek*. I look at them and all I can think is, Dear God, where did she go? What did that woman do to her? Then I feel sick and sorry. She was so pretty, with pink cheeks and bright brown eyes, and her hair the shade of blonde you know will darken and get mousy. Sweet is the only word that fits. Sweet and bright and innocent. Her mother's sickness hadn't touched her very deeply, not then.

'I kind of started up awake and tried to smile. It was hard to think what to do. I was logy from the sun and my mind felt sticky and slow. I said "Hi." She was wearing a little yellow dress, sort of cute but awfully long for a little girl in the summer. It came down to her shins.

'She didn't smile back. She just pointed and said, "What are those?"

'I looked down and saw that my top had slipped while I was asleep. So I fixed it and said, "Those are my breasts, Carrie."

'Then she said—very solemnly: "I wish I had some."

'I said: "You have to wait, Carrie. You won't start to get them for another . . . oh, eight or nine years."

32

' "No, I won't," she said. "Momma says good girls don't." She looked strange for a little girl, half sad and half self-righteous.

'I could hardly believe it, and the first thing that popped into my mind also popped right out of my mouth. I said: "Well, I'm a good girl. And doesn't your mother have breasts?"

'She lowered her head and said something so softly I couldn't hear it. When I asked her to repeat it, she looked at me defiantly and said that her momma had been bad when she made her and that was why she had them. She called them dirtypillows, as if it was all one word.

'I couldn't believe it. I was just dumbfounded. There was nothing at all I could think to say. We just stared at each other, and what I wanted to do was grab that sad little scrap of a girl and run away with her.

'And that was when Margaret White came out of her back door and saw us.

'For a minute she just goggled as if she couldn't believe it. Then she opened her mouth and whooped. That's the ugliest sound I've ever heard in my life. It was like the noise of a bull alligator would make in a swamp. She just *whooped*. Rage. Complete, insane rage. Her face went just as red as the side of a fire truck and she curled her hands into fists and whooped at the sky. She was shaking all over. I thought she was having a stroke. Her face was all scrunched up, and it was a gargoyle's face.

'I thought Carrie was going to faint—or die on the spot. She sucked in all her breath and that little face went a cottage-cheesy colour.

'Her mother yelled: "CAAAARRRIEEEEEE!"

'I jumped up and yelled back: "Don't you yell at her that way! You ought to be ashamed!" Something stupid like that. I don't remember. Carrie started to go back and then she stopped and then she started again, and just before she crossed over from our lawn to theirs she looked back at me and there was a look . . . oh, dreadful. I can't say it. Wanting and hating and fearing . . . and *misery*. As if life itself had fallen on her like stones, all at the age of three.

'My mother came out on the back stoop and her face just crumpled when she saw the child. And Margaret . . . oh, she was screaming things about sluts and strumpets and the sins of the fathers being visited even into the seventh generation. My tongue felt like a little dried-up plant.

'For just a second Carrie stood swaying back and forth between the two yards, and then Margaret White looked upward and I swear sweet Jesus that woman *bayed* at the sky. And then she started to . . . to hurt herself, scourge herself. She was clawing at her neck and cheeks, making red marks and scratches. She tore her dress.

'Carrie screamed out "Momma!" and ran to her.

'Mrs White kind of . . . squatted, like a frog, and her arms swooped wide open. I thought she was going to crush her and I screamed. The woman was grinning. Grinning and drooling right down her chin. Oh, I was sick. Jesus, I was so sick.

'She gathered her up and they went in. I turned off my radio and I could hear her. Some of the words, but not all. You didn't have to hear all the words to know what was going on. Praying and sobbing and screeching. Crazy sounds. And Margaret telling the little girl to get herself into her closet and pray. The little girl crying and screaming that she was sorry, she forgot. Then nothing. And my mother and I just looked at each other. I never saw Mom look so bad, not even when Dad died. She said: "The child—" and that was all. We went inside.'

She gets up and goes to the window, a pretty woman in a yellow no-back sundress. 'It's almost like living it all over again, you know,' she says, not turning around. 'I'm all riled up inside again.' She laughs a little and cradles her elbows in her palms.

'Oh, she was so pretty. You'd never know from those pictures.'

Cars go by outside, back and forth, and I sit and wait for her to go on. She reminds me of a pole-vaulter eyeing the bar and wondering if it's set too high.

'My mother brewed us scotch tea, strong, with milk, the way she used to when I was tomboying around and someone would push me in the nettle patch or I'd fall off my bicycle. It was awful but we drank it anyway, sitting across from each other in the kitchen nook. She was in some old housedress with the hem falling down in back, and I was in my Whore of Babylon two-piece swimsuit. I wanted to cry but it was too real to cry about, not like the movies. Once when I was in New York I saw an old drunk leading a little girl in a blue dress by the hand. The girl had cried herself into a bloody nose. The drunk had goitre and his neck looked like an inner tube. There was a red bump in the middle of his forehead and a long white string on the blue serge jacket he was wearing. Everyone kept going and coming because, if you did, then pretty soon you wouldn't see them any more. That was real, too.

'I wanted to tell my mother that, and I was just opening my mouth to say it when the other thing happened . . . the thing you want to hear about, I guess. There was a big thump outside that made the glasses rattle in the china cabinet. It was a feeling as well as a sound, thick and solid, as if someone had just pushed an iron safe off the roof.'

She lights a new cigarette and begins to puff rapidly.

'I went to the window and looked out, but I couldn't see anything. Then, when I was getting ready to turn around, something else fell. The sun glittered on it. I thought it was a big glass globe for a second. Then it hit the edge of the

Whites' roof and shattered, and it wasn't glass at all. It was a big chunk of ice. I was going to turn around and tell Mom, and that's when they started to fall all at once, in a shower.

'They were falling on the Whites' roof, on the back and front lawn, on the outside door to their cellar. That was a sheet-tin bulkhead, and when the first one hit it made a huge *bong* noise, like a church bell. My mother and I both screamed. We were clutching each other like a couple of girls in a thunderstorm.

'Then it stopped. There was no sound at all from their house. You could see the water from the melting ice trickling down their slate shingles in the sunshine. A great big hunk of ice was stuck in the angle of the roof and their little chimney. The light on it was so bright that my eyes hurt to look at it.

'My mother started to ask me if it was over, and then Margaret screamed. The sound came to us very clearly. In a way it was worse than before, because there was terror in this one. Then there were clanging, banging sounds, as if she were throwing every pot and pan in the house at the girl.

The back door slammed open and slammed closed. No one came out. More screams. Mom said for me to call the police but I couldn't move. I was stuck to the spot. Mr Kirk and his wife Virginia came out on their lawn to look. The Smiths, too. Pretty soon everyone on the street that was home had come out, even old Mrs Warwick from up the block, and she was deaf in one ear.

'Things started to crash and tinkle and break. Bottles, glasses, I don't know what all. And then the side window broke open and the kitchen table fell halfway through. With God as my witness. It was a big mahogany thing and it took the screen with it and it must have weighed three hundred pounds. How could a woman—even a big

36

woman—throw that?'

I ask her if she is implying something.

'I'm only *telling* you,' she insists, suddenly distraught. 'I'm not asking you to believe—'

She seems to catch her breath and then goes on flatly:

'There was nothing for maybe five minutes. Water was dripping out of the gutters over there. And there was ice all over the Whites' lawn. It was melting fast.'

She gives a short, chopping laugh and butts her cigarette.

'Why not? It *was* August.'

She wanders aimlessly back towards the sofa, then veers away. 'Then the stones. Right out of the blue sky. Whistling and screaming like bombs. My mother cried out, "What, in the name of God!" and put her hands over her head. But I couldn't move. I watched it all and I couldn't move. It didn't matter anyway. They only fell on the Whites' property.

'One of them hit a downspout and knocked it on to the lawn. Others punched holes right through the roof and into the attic. The roof made a big cracking sound each time one hit, and puffs of dust would squirt up. The ones that hit the ground made everything vibrate. You could feel them hitting in your feet.

'Our china was tinkling and the fancy Welsh dresser was shaking and Mom's teacup fell on the floor and broke.

'They made big pits in the Whites' back lawn when they struck. Craters. Mrs White hired a junkman from across-town to cart them away, and Jerry Smith from up the street paid him a buck to let him chip a piece of one. He took it to B.U. and they looked at it and said it was ordinary granite.

'One of the last ones hit a little table they had in their back yard and smashed it to pieces.

37

'But nothing, nothing that wasn't on their property was hit.'

She stops and turns from the window to look at me, and her face is haggard from remembering all that. One hand plays forgetfully with her casually stylish shag haircut. 'Not much of it got into the local paper. By the time Billy Harris came around—he reported the Chamberlain news—she had already gotten the roof fixed, and when people told him the stones had gone right through it, I think he thought we were pulling his leg.

'Nobody wants to believe it, not even now. You and all the people who'll read what you write will wish they could laugh it off and call me just another nut who's been out here in the sun too long. But it *happened*. There were lots of people on the block who *saw* it happen, and it was just as real as that drunk leading the little girl with the bloody nose. And now there's this other thing. No one can laugh that off, either. Too many people are dead.

'And it's not just on the Whites' property any more.'

She smiles, but there's not a drop of humour in it. She says: 'Ralph White was insured, and Margaret got a lot of money when he died . . . double indemnity. He left the house insured, too, but she never got a penny of that. The damage was caused by an act of God. Poetic justice, huh?'

She laughs a little, but there's no humour in that, either . . .

Found written repeatedly on one page of a Ewen Consolidated High School notebook owned by Carrie White:

Everybody's guessed/that baby can't be blessed/'til she finally sees that she's like all the rest . . .

*

Carrie went into the house and closed the door behind her. Bright daylight disappeared and was replaced by brown shadows, coolness, and the oppressive smell of talcum powder. The only sound was the ticking of the Black Forest cuckoo clock in the living room. Momma had gotten the cuckoo clock with Green Stamps. Once, in the sixth grade, Carrie had set out to ask Momma if Green Stamps weren't sinful, but her nerve had failed her.

She walked up the hall and put her coat in the closet. A luminous picture above the coathooks limned a ghostly Jesus hovering grimly over a family seated at the kitchen table. Beneath was the caption (also luminous): *The Unseen Guest*.

She went into the living room and stood in the middle of the faded, starting-to-be-threadbare rug. She closed her eyes and watched the little dots flash by in the darkness. Her headache thumped queasily behind her temples.

Alone.

Momma worked on the speed ironer and folder down at the Blue Ribbon Laundry in Chamberlain Centre. She had worked there since Carrie was five, when the compensation and insurance that had resulted from her father's accident had begun to run out. Her hours were from seven-thirty in the morning until four in the afternoon. The laundry was Godless. Momma had told her so many times. The foreman, Mr Elton Mott, was especially Godless. Momma said that Satan had reserved a special blue corner of Hell for Elt, as he was called at the Blue Ribbon.

Alone.

She opened her eyes. The living room contained two chairs with straight backs. There was a sewing table with a light where Carrie sometimes made dresses in the evening while Momma tatted doilies and talked about The Coming. The Black Forest cuckoo clock was on the far wall.

39

There were many religious pictures, but the one Carrie liked best was on the wall above her chair. It was Jesus leading lambs on a hill that was as green and smooth as the Riverside golf course. The others were not as tranquil: Jesus turning the money-changers from the temple, Moses throwing the Tablets down upon the worshippers of the golden calf, Thomas the Doubter putting his hand on Christ's wounded side (oh, the horrified fascination of that one and the nightmares it had given her as a girl!), Noah's ark floating above the agonined, drowning sinners, Lot and his family fleeing the great burning of Sodom and Gomorrah.

On a small deal table there were a lamp and a stack of tracts. The top pamphlet showed a sinner (his spiritual status was obvious from the agonized expression on his face) trying to crawl beneath a large boulder. The title blared: *Neither shall the rock hide him ON THAT DAY!*

But the room was actually dominated by a huge plaster crucifix on the far wall, fully four feet high. Momma had mail-ordered it special from St Louis. The Jesus impaled upon it was frozen in a grotesque, muscle-straining rictus of pain, mouth drawn down in a groaning curve. His crown of thorns bled scarlet streams down temples and forehead. The eyes were turned up in a medieval expression of slanted agony. Both hands were also drenched with blood and the feet were nailed to a small plaster platform. This corpus had also given Carrie endless nightmares in which the mutilated Christ chased her through dream corridors, holding a mallet and nails, begging her to take up her cross and follow Him. Just lately these dreams had evolved into something less understandable but more sinister. The object did not seem to be murder but something even more awful.

Alone.

The pain in her legs and belly and privates had drained

away a little. She no longer thought she was bleeding to death. The word was *menstruation*, and all at once it seemed logical and inevitable. It was her Time of the Month. She giggled a strange, affrighted giggle in the solemn stillness of the living room. It sounded like a quiz show. You too can win an all-expenses-paid trip to Bermuda on Time of the Month. Like the memory of the stones, the knowledge of menstruation seemed always to have been there, blocked but waiting.

She turned and walked heavily upstairs. The bathroom had a wooden floor that had been scrubbed nearly white (Cleanliness is next to Godliness) and a tub on claw feet. Rust stains dripped down the porcelain below the chrome spout, and there was no shower attachment. Momma said showers were sinful.

Carrie went in, opened the towel cabinet, and began to hunt purposefully but carefully, not leaving anything out of place. Momma's eyes were sharp.

The blue box was in the very back, behind the old towels they didn't use any more. There was a fuzzily silhouetted woman in a long, filmy gown on the side.

She took one of the napkins out and looked at it curiously. She had blotted the lipstick she stuck into her purse quite openly with these—once on a street corner. Now she remembered (or imagined she did) quizzical, shocked looks. Her face flamed. *They* had told her. The flush faded to a milky anger.

She went into her tiny bedroom. There were many more religious pictures here, but there were more lambs and fewer scenes of righteous wrath. A Ewen pennant was tacked over the dresser. On the dresser itself was a Bible and a plastic Jesus that glowed in the dark.

She undressed—first her blouse, then her hateful knee-length skirt, her slip, her girdle, her pettipants, her garter belt, her stockings, She looked at the pile of heavy clothes,

41

their buttons and rubber, with an expression of fierce wretchedness. In the school library there was a stack of back issues of *Seventeen* and often she leafed through them, pasting an expression of idiotic casualness on her face. The models looked so easy and smooth in their short, kicky skirts, pantyhose, and frilly underwear with patterns on them. Of course *easy* was one of Momma's pet words (she knew what Momma would say to a question) to describe *them*. And it would make her dreadfully self-conscious, she knew that. Naked, evil, blackened with the sin of exhibitionism, the breeze blowing lewdly up the backs of her legs, inciting lust. And she knew that *they* would know how she felt. They always did. They would embarrass her somehow, push her savagely back into clowndom. It was their way.

She could, she knew she could be

(what)

in another place. She was thick through the waist only because sometimes she felt so miserable, empty, bored, that the only way to fill that gaping, whistling hole was to eat and eat and eat—but she was not *that* thick through the middle. Her body chemistry would not allow her to go beyond a certain point. And she thought her legs were actually pretty, almost as pretty as Sue Snell's or Vicky Hanscom's. She could be

(what o what o what)

could stop the chocolates and her pimples would go down. They always did. She could fix her hair. Buy pantyhose and blue and green tights. Make little skirts and dresses from Butterick and Simplicity patterns. The price of a bus ticket, a train ticket. She could be, could be, could *be*—

Alive.

She unsnapped her heavy cotton bra and let it fall. Her breasts were milk-white, upright and smooth. The nipples

42

were a light coffee colour. She ran her hands over them and a little shiver went through her. Evil, bad, oh it was. Momma had told her there was Something. The Something was dangerous, ancient, unutterably evil. It could make you Feeble. *Watch*, Momma said. *It comes at night. It will make you think of the evil that goes on in parking lots and roadhouses.*

But, though this was only nine-twenty in the morning, Carrie thought that the Something had come to her. She ran her hands over her breasts

(dirtypillows)

again, and the skin was cool but the nipples were hot and hard, and when she tweaked one it made her feel weak and dissolving. Yes, this was the Something.

Her underpants were spotted with blood.

Suddenly she felt that she must burst into tears, scream, or rip the Something out of her body whole and, beating, crush it, kill it.

The napkin Miss Desjardin had fixed was already wilting and she changed it carefully, knowing how bad she was, how bad *they* were, how she hated them and herself. Only Momma was good. Momma had battled the Black Man and had vanquished him. Carrie had seen it happen in a dream. Momma had driven him out of the front door with a broom, and the Black Man had fled up Carlin Street into the night, his cloven feet striking red sparks from the cement.

Her momma had torn the Something out of herself and was pure.

Carrie hated her.

She caught a glimpse of her own face in the tiny mirror she had hung on the back of the door, a mirror with a cheap green plastic rim, good only for combing hair by.

She hated her face, her dull, stupid, bovine face, the vapid eyes, the red, shiny pimples, the nests of blackheads. She hated her face most of all.

The reflection was suddenly split by a jagged, silvery crack. The mirror fell on the floor and shattered at her feet, leaving only the plastic ring to stare at her like a blinded eye.

From *Ogilvie's Dictionary of Physic Phenomena:*

Telekinesis is the ability to move objects or to cause changes in objects by force of the mind. The phenomenon has most reliably been reported in times of crisis or in stress situations, when automobiles have been levitated from pinned bodies or debris from collapsed buildings, etc.

The phenomenon is often confused with the work of *poltergeists,* which are playful spirits. It should be noted that poltergeists are astral beings of questionable reality, while telekinesis is thought to be an empiric function of the mind, possibly electrochemical in nature . . .

When they had finished making love, as she slowly put her clothes in order in the back seat of Tommy Ross's 1963 Ford, Sue Snell found her thoughts turning back to Carrie White.

It was Friday night and Tommy (who was still looking pensively out the back window with his pants still down around his ankles; the effect was comic but oddly endearing) had taken her bowling. That, of course, was a mutually accepted excuse. Fornication had been on their minds from the word go.

She had been going out more or less steadily with Tommy ever since October (it was now May) and they had been lovers for only two weeks. Seven times, she amended. Tonight had been the seventh. There had been no fireworks yet, no bands playing 'Stars and Stripes

Forever,' but it had gotten a little better.

The first time had hurt like hell. Her girl friends, Helen Shyres and Jeanne Gault, had both done It, and they both assured her that it only hurt for a minute—like getting a shot of penicillin—and then it was roses. But for Sue, the first time had been like being reamed out with a hoe handle. Tommy had confessed to her since, with a grin, that he had gotten the rubber on wrong, too.

Tonight was only the second time she had begun to feel something like pleasure, and then it was over. Tommy had held out for as long as he could, but then it was just . . . over. It seemed like an awful lot of rubbing for a little warmth.

In the aftermath she felt low and melancholy, and her thoughts turned to Carrie in this light. A wave of remorse caught her with all emotional guards down, and when Tommy turned back from the view of Brickyard Hill, she was crying.

'Hey,' he said, alarmed. 'Oh, hey.' He held her clumsily.

' 'S all right,' she said still weeping. 'It's not you. I did a not-so-good thing today. I was just thinking of it.'

'What?' He patted the back of her neck gently.

So she found herself launching into the story of that morning's incident, hardly believing it was herself she was listening to. Facing the thing frankly, she realized the main reason she had allowed Tommy to have her was because she was in

(love? infatuation? didn't matter results were the same) with him, and now to put herself in this position—cohort in a nasty shower-room joke—was hardly the approved method to hook a fellow. And Tommy was, of course, Popular. As someone who had been Popular herself all her life, it had almost seemed written that she would meet and fall in love with someone as Popular as she. They were almost certain to be voted King and Queen of the high

45

school Spring Ball, and the senior class had already voted them class couple for the yearbook. They had become a fixed star in the shifting firmament of the high school's relationships, the acknowledged Romeo and Juliet. And she knew with sudden hatefulness that there was one couple like them in every white suburban high school in America.

And having something she had always longed for—a sense of place, of security, of status—she found that it carried uneasiness with it like a darker sister. It was not the way she had conceived it. There were dark things lumbering around their warm circle of light. The idea that she had let him fuck her

(do you have to say it that way yes this time I do)

simply because he was Popular, for instance. The fact that they fit together walking, or that she could look at their reflection in a store window and think. *There goes a handsome couple*. She was quite sure

(or only hopeful)

that she wasn't that weak, not that liable to fall docilely into the complacent expectations of parents, friends, and even herself. But now there was this shower thing, where she had gone along and pitched in with high, savage glee. The word she was avoiding was expressed *To Conform,* in the infinitive, and it conjured up miserable images of hair in rollers, long afternoons in front of the ironing board in front of the soap operas while hubby was off busting heavies in an anonymous Office; of joining the P.T.A. and then the country club when their income moved into five figures; of pills in circular yellow cases without number to insure against having to move out of the misses' size before it became absolutely necessary and against the intrusion of repulsive little strangers who shat in their pants and screamed for help at two in the morning; of fighting with desperate decorum to keep the niggers out of

Kleen Korners, standing shoulder to shoulder with Terri Smith (Miss Potato Blossom of 1975) and Vicki Jones (Vice President of The Women's League), armed with signs and petitions and sweet, slightly desperate smiles.

Carrie, it was the goddamned Carrie, this was her fault. Perhaps before today she had heard distant, circling footfalls around their lighted place, but tonight, hearing her own sordid, crummy story, she saw the actual silhouettes of all these things, and yellow eyes that glowed like flashlights in the dark.

She had already bought her prom gown. It was blue. It was beautiful.

'You're right,' he said when she was done. 'Bad news. Doesn't sound a bit like you.' His face was grave and she felt a cool slice of terror. Then he smiled—he had a very jolly smile—and the darknesss retreated a bit.

'I kicked a kid in the slats once when he was knocked out. Did I ever tell you about that?'

She shook her head.

'Yeah.' He rubbed his nose reminiscently and his cheek gave a small tic, the way it had when he made his confession about getting the rubber wrong the first time. 'The kid's name was Danny Patrick. He beat the living shit out of me once when we were in the sixth grade. I hated him, but I was scared, too. I was laying for him. You know how that is?'

She didn't, but nodded anyway.

'Anyway, he finally picked on the wrong kid a year or so later. Pete Taber. He was just a little guy, but he had lots of muscles. Danny got on him about something. I don't know, marbles or something, and finally Peter just rose up righteous and beat the shit out of him. That was on the playground of the old Kennedy Junior High. Danny fell down and hit his head and went out cold. Everybody ran. We thought he might be dead. I ran away too, but first I gave him a good kick in the ribs. Felt really bad about it afterwards. You going to apologize to her?'

It caught Sue flat-footed and all she could was clinch weakly: 'Did you?'

'Huh? Hell no! I had better things to do than spend my time in traction. But there's a big difference, Susie.'

'There is?'

'It's not seventh grade any more. And I had some kind of reason, even if it was a piss-poor reason. What did that sad, silly bitch ever do to you?'

She didn't answer because she couldn't. She had never passed more than a hundred words with Carrie in her whole life, and three dozen or so had come today. Phys. Ed. was the only class they'd had in common since they had graduated from Chamberlain Junior High. Carrie was taking the commercial/business course. Sue, of course, was in the college division.

She thought herself suddenly loathsome.

She found she could not bear that and so she twisted it at him. 'When did you start making all these big moral decisions? After you started fucking me?'

She saw the good humour fade from his face and was sorry.

'Guess I should have kept quiet,' he said, and pulled up his pants.

'It's not you, it's me.' She put a hand on his arm. 'I'm ashamed, see?'

'I know,' he said. 'But I shouldn't be giving advice. I'm not very good at it.'

'Tommy, do you ever hate being so . . . well, Popular?'

'Me?' The question wrote surprise on his face. 'Do you mean like football and class president and that stuff?'

'Yes.'

'No. It's not very important. High school isn't a very important place. When you're going you think it's a big

48

deal, but when it's over nobody really thinks it was great unless they're beered up. That's how my brother and his buddies are, anyway.'

It did not soothe her; it made her fears worse. Little Susie mix 'n match from Ewen High School, Head Cupcake of the entire Cupcake Brigade. Prom gown kept forever in the closet, wrapped in protective plastic.

The night pressed dark against the slightly steamed car windows.

'I'll probably end up working at my dad's car lot,' he said. 'I'll spend my Friday and Saturday nights down at Uncle Billy's or out at The Cavalier drinking beer and talking about the Saturday afternoon I got that fat pitch from Saunders and we upset Dorchester. Get married to some nagging broad and always own last year's model, vote Democrat—'

'Don't,' she said, her mouth suddenly full of a dark, sweet horror. She pulled him to her. 'Love me. My head is so bad tonight. Love me. Love me.'

So he loved her and this time it was different, this time there finally seemed to be room and there was no tiresome rubbing but a delicious friction that went up and up: Twice he had to stop, panting, and held himself back, and then he went again

(he was a virgin before me and admitted it I would have believed a lie)

and went hard and her breath came in short, digging gasps and then she began to yell and hold at his back, helpless to stop, sweating, the bad taste washed away, every cell seeming to have its own climax, body filled with sunlight, musical notes in her mind, butterflies behind her skull in the cage of her mind.

Later, on the way home, he asked her formally if she would go to the Spring Ball with him. She said she would. He asked her if she had decided what to do about Carrie.

49

She said she hadn't. He said that it made no difference, but she thought that it did. It had begun to seem that it meant all the difference.

From *Telekinesis: Analysis and Aftermath* (Science Yearbook 1982), by Dean K. L. McGuffin:

There are, of course, still these scientists today—regretfully, the Duke University people are in their forefront—who reject the terrific underlying implications of the Carrie White affair. Like the Flatlands Society, the Rosicrucians, or the Corlies of Arizona, who are positive that the atomic bomb does not work, these unfortunates are flying in the face of logic with their heads in the sand—and beg your pardon for the mixed metaphor.

Of course one is able to understand the consternation, the raised voices, the angry letters and arguments at scientific convocations. The idea of telekinesis itself has been a bitter pill for the scientific community to swallow, with its horror-movie trappings of ouija boards and mediums and table rappings and floating coronets; but understanding will still not excuse scientific irresponsibility.

The outcome of the White affair raises grave and difficult questions. An earthquake has struck our order notions of the way the natural world is supposed to act and react. Can you blame even such a renowned physicist as Gerald Luponet for claiming the whole thing is a hoax and a fraud, even in the face of such overwhelming evidence as the White Commission presented? For if Carrie White is the truth, then what of Newton? . . .

They sat in the living room, Carrie and Momma, listening to Tennessee Ernie Ford singing 'Let the Lower Lights Be Burning' on a Webcor phonograph (which Momma called the victrola, or, if in a particularly good mood, the vic). Carrie sat at the sewing machine, pumping with her feet as she sewed the sleeves on a new dress. Momma sat beneath the plaster crucifix, tatting doilies and bumping her feet in time to the song, which was one of her favourites. Mr P. P. Bliss, who had written this hymn and others seemingly without number, was one of Momma's shining examples of God at work upon the face of the earth. He had been a sailor and a sinner (two terms that were synonymous in Momma's lexicon), a great blasphemer, a laugher in the face of the Almighty. Then a great storm had come up at sea, the boat had threatened to capsize, and Mr P. P. Bliss had gotten down on his sinsickly knees with a vision of Hell yawning beneath the ocean floor to receive him, and he had prayed to God. Mr P. P. Bliss promised God that if He saved him, he would dedicate the rest of his life to Him. The storm, of course, had cleared immediately.

> *Brightly beams our Father's mercy*
> *From his lighthouse evermore,*
> *But to us he gives the keeping*
> *Of the lights along the shore . . .*

All of Mr P. P. Bloss's hymns had a seagoing flavour to them.

The dress she was sewing was actually quite pretty, a dark wine colour—the closest Momma would allow her to red—and the sleeves were puffed. She tried to keep her mind strictly on her sewing, but of course it wandered.

The overhead light was strong and harsh and yellow, the small dusty plush sofa was of course deserted (Carrie had never had a boy in To Sit), and on the far wall was a twin shadow: the crucified Jesus, and beneath Him, Momma.

The school had called Momma at the laundry and she

had come home at noon. Carrie had watched her come up the walk, and her belly trembled.

Momma was a very big woman, and she always wore a hat. Lately her legs had begun to swell, and her feet always seemed on the point of overflowing her shoes. She wore a black cloth coat with a black fur collar. Her eyes were blue and magnified behind rimless bifocals. She always carried a large black satchel purse and in it was her change purse, her billfold (both black), a large King James Bible (also black) with her name stamped on the front in gold, and a stack of tracts secured with a rubber band. The Tracts were usually orange, and smearily printed.

Carrie knew vaguely that Momma and Daddy Ralph had been Baptists once but had left the church when they became convinced that the Baptists were doing the work of the Antichrist. Since that time, all worship had taken place at home. Momma held worship on Sundays, Tuesdays, and Fridays. These were called Holy Days.

Momma was the minister, Carrie the congregation. Services lasted from two to three hours.

Momma had opened the door and walked stolidly in. She and Carrie had stared at each other down the short length of the front hall for a moment, like gunfighters before a shootout. It was one of those brief moments that seem

(fear could it really have been fear in momma's eyes)

much longer in retrospect.

Momma closed the door behind her. 'You're a woman,' she said softly.

Carrie felt her face twisting and crumpling and could not help it. 'Why didn't you *tell* me?' she cried. 'Oh Momma, I was so *scared!* And the girls all made fun and threw things and—'

Momma had been walking towards her, and now her hand flashed with sudden limber speed, a hard hand, laundry-calloused and muscled. It struck her backhand across the jaw and Carrie fell down in the doorway between the hall and the living room, weeping loudly.

'And God made Eve from the rib of Adam,' Momma said. Her eyes were very large in the rimless glasses; they looked like poached eggs. She thumped Carrie with the side of her foot and Carrie screamed. 'Get up, woman. Let's get in and pray. Let's pray to Jesus for our woman-weak, wicked, sinning souls.'

'*Momma*'—

The sobs were too strong to allow more. The latent hysterics had come out grinning and gibbering. She could not stand up. She could only crawl into the living room with her hair hanging in her face, braying huge hoarse sobs. Every now and again Momma would swing her foot. So they progressed across the living room toward the place of the altar, which had once been a small bedroom.

'And Eve was weak and—say it, woman. Say it!'

'No, Momma, please help me—'

The foot swung. Carrie screamed.

'And Eve was weak and loosed the raven on the world,' Momma continued, 'and the raven was called Sin, and the first Sin was Intercourse. And the Lord visited Eve with a Curse, and the Curse was the Curse of Blood. And Adam and Eve were driven out of the Garden and into the World and Eve found that her belly had grown big with child.'

The foot swung and connected with Carrie's rump. Her nose scraped the wood floor. They were entering the place of the altar. There was a cross on a table covered with an embroidered silk cloth. On either side of the cross there were white candles. Behind this were several paint-by-the-numbers of Jesus and His apostles. And to the right was the worst place of all, the home of terror, the cave where all hope, all resistance to God's will—and Momma's—

was extinguished. The closet door leered open. Inside, below a hideous blue bulb that was always lit, was Derrault's conception of Jonathan Edwards' famous sermon. *Sinners in the Hands of an Angry God.*

'And there was a second Curse, and this was the Curse of Childbearing, and Eve brought forth Cain in sweat and blood.'

Now Momma dragged her, half-standing and half-crawling, down to the altar, where they both fell on their knees. Momma gripped Carrie's wrist tightly.

'And following Cain, Eve gave birth to Abel, having not yet repented of the Sin of Intercourse. And so the Lord visited Eve with a third Curse, and this was the Curse of Murder. Cain rose up and slew Abel with a rock. And still Eve did not repent, nor all the daughters of Eve, and upon Eve did the Crafty Serpent found a kingdom of whoredom and pestilences.'

'Momma!' she shrieked. 'Momma, please listen! *It wasn't my fault!'*

'Bow your head,' Momma said. 'Let's us pray.'

'You should have told me!'

Momma brought her hand down on the back of Carrie's neck, and behind it was all the heavy muscle developed by eleven years of slinging heavy laundry bags and trucking piles of wet sheets. Carrie's eye-bulging face jerked forward and her forehead smacked the altar, leaving a mark and making the candles tremble.

'Let's us pray,' Momma said softly, implacably.

Weeping and snuffling, Carrie bowed her head. A runner of snot hung pendulously from her nose and she wiped it away.

(if i had a nickel for every time she made me cry here)

with the back of her hand.

'O Lord,' Momma declaimed hugely, her head thrown back, 'help this sinning woman beside me here see the sin of her days and ways. Show her that if she had remained sinless the Curse of Blood never would have come on her. She may have committed the Sin of Lustful Thoughts. She may have been listening to rock 'n roll music on the radio. She may have been tempted by the Antichrist. Show her that this is Your kind, vengeful hand at work and—'

'No! Let me go!'

She tried to struggle to her feet and Momma's hand, as strong and pitiless as an iron manacle, forced her back to her knees.

'—and Your sign that she must walk the straight and narrow from here on out if she is to avoid the flaming agonies of the Eternal Pit. Amen.'

She turned her glittering, magnified eyes upon her daughter. 'Go to your closet now.'

'No!' She felt her breath go thick with terror.

'Go to your closet. Pray in secret. Ask forgiveness for your sins.'

'I didn't sin, Momma. *You* sinned. You didn't tell me and they laughed.'

Again she seemed to see a flash of fear in Momma's eyes, gone as quickly and soundlessly as summer lightning. Momma began to force Carrie toward the blue glare of the closet.

'Pray to God and your sins may be washed away.'

'Momma, you let me go.'

'Pray, woman.'

'I'll make the stones come again, Momma.'

Momma halted.

Even her breath seemed to stop in her throat for a moment. And then the hand tightened on her neck, tightened, until Carrie saw red, lurid dots in front of her eyes and felt her brain go fuzzy and far-off.

Momma's magnified eyes swam in front of her.

55

'You spawn of the devil,' she whispered. 'Why was I so cursed?'

Carrie's whirling mind strove to find something huge enough to express her agony, shame, terror, hate, fear. It seemed her whole life had narrowed to this miserable, beaten point of rebellion. Her eyes bulged crazily, her mouth, filled with spit, opened wide.

'YOU SUCK!' she screamed.

Momma hissed like a burned cat. 'Sin!' she cried. 'O, Sin! She began to beat Carrie's back, her neck, her head. Carrie was driven, reeling, into the close blue glare of the closet.

'YOU FUCK!' Carrie screamed.

(there there o there it's out how else do you think she got you o god o good)

She was whirled into the closet headfirst and she struck the far wall and fell on the floor in a semidaze. The door slammed and the key turned.

She was alone with Momma's angry God.

The blue light glared on a picture of a huge and bearded Yahweh who was casting screaming multitudes of humans down through cloudy depths into an abyss of fire. Below them, black horrid figures struggled through the flames of perdition while The Black Man sat on a huge flame-coloured throne with a trident in one hand. His body was that of a man, but he had a spiked tail and the head of a jackal.

She would not break this time.

But of course she did break. It took six hours but she broke, weeping and calling Momma to open the door and let her out. The need to urinate was terrible. The Black Man grinned at her with his jackal mouth, and his scarlet eyes knew all the secrets of woman-blood.

An hour after Carrie began to call, Momma let her out. Carrie scrabbled madly for the bathroom.

It was only now, three hours after that, sitting here with her head bowed over the sewing machine like a penitent, that she remembered the fear in Momma's eyes and she thought she knew the reason why.

There had been other times when Momma had kept her in the closet for as long as a day at a stretch—when she stole that forty-nine-cent finger ring from Shuber's Five and Ten, the time she had found that picture of Flash Bobby Pickett under Carrie's pillow—and Carrie had once fainted from the lack of food and the smell of her own waste. And she had never, never spoken back as she had done today. Today she had even said the Eff Word. Yet Momma had let her out almost as soon as she broke.

There. The dress was done. She removed her feet from the treadle and held it up to look at it. It was long. And ugly. She hated it.

She knew why Momma had let her out.

'Momma, may I go to bed?'

'Yes.' Momma did not look up from her doily.

She folded the dress over her arm. She looked down at the sewing machine. All at once the treadle depressed itself. The needle began to dip up and down, catching the light in steely flashes. The bobbin whirred and jerked. The sidewheel spun.

Momma's head jerked up, her eyes wide. The looped matrix at the edge of her doily, wonderfully intricate yet at the same time as precise and even, suddenly fell in disarray.

'Only clearing the thread,' Carrie said softly.

'Go to bed,' Momma said curtly, and the fear was back in her eyes.

'Yes,

(she was afraid i'd knock the closet door right off its hinges)

Momma,'

57

(and i think i could i think i could yes i think i could)

From *The Shadow Exploded* (p. 58):

Margaret White was born and raised in Motton, a small town which borders Chamberlain and sends its tuition students to Chamberlain's junior and senior high schools. Her parents were fairly well-to-do; they owned a prosperous night spot just outside the Motton town limits called The Jolly Roadhouse. Margaret's father, John Brigham, was killed in a barroom shooting incident in the summer of 1959.

Margaret Brigham, who was then almost thirty, began attending fundamentalist prayer meetings. Her mother had become involved with a new man (Harold Alison, whom she later married) and they both wanted Margaret out of the house—she believed her mother, Judith, and Harold Alison were living in sin and made her views known frequently. Judith Brigham expected her daughter to remain a spinster the rest of her life. In the more pungent phraseology of her soon-to-be stepfather, 'Margaret had a face like the ass end of a gasoline truck and a body to match.' He also referred to her as 'a little prayin' Jesus.'

Margaret refused to leave until 1960, when she met Ralph White at a revival meeting. In September of that year she left the Brigham residence in Motton and moved to a small flat in Chamberlain Centre.

The courtship of Margaret Brigham and Ralph White terminated in marriage on March 23, 1962. On April 3, 1962, Margaret White was admitted briefly to Westover Doctors Hospital.

'Nope, she wouldn't tell us what was wrong,' Harold Alison said. 'The one time we went to see her she told us we were living in adultery even though we were hitched, and we were going to hell. She said God had put an invisible mark on our foreheads, but she could see it. Acted crazy as a bat in a henhouse, she did. Her mom tried to be nice, tried to find out what the matter with her was. She got hysterical and started to rave about an angel with a sword who would walk through the parking lots of roadhouses and cut down the wicked. We left.'

Judith Alison, however, had at least an idea of what might have been wrong with her daughter; she thought that Margaret had gone through a miscarriage. If so, the baby was conceived out of wedlock. Confirmation of this would shed an interesting light on the character of Carrie's mother.

In a long and rather hysterical letter to her mother dated August 19, 1962, Margaret said that she and Ralph were living sinlessly, without 'the Curse of Intercourse'. She urged Harold and Judith Alison to close their 'abode of wickedness' and do likewise. 'It is,' Margaret declares near the end of her letter, 'the only [sic] way you & That Man can avoid the Rain of Blood yet to come. Ralph & I, like Mary & Joseph, will neither know or polute [sic] each other's flesh. If there is issue, let it be Divine.'

Of course, the calendar tells us that Carrie was conceived later that same year . . .

The girls dressed quietly for their Monday morning Period One gym class, with no horseplay or little screaming catcalls, and none of them were very surprised when Miss Desjardin slammed open the locker-room and walked in. Her silver whistle dangling between her small breasts, and if her shorts were the ones she had been wearing on Friday, no trace of Carrie's bloody handprint remained.

The girls continued to dress sullenly, not looking at her.

'Aren't you the bunch to send out for graduation,' Miss

Desjardin said softly. 'When is it? A month? And the Spring Ball even less than that. Most of you have your dates and gowns already, I bet. Sue, you'll be going with Tommy Ross. Helen, Roy Evarts. Chris, I imagine you can take your pick. Who's the lucky guy?'

'Billy Nolan,' Chris Hargensen said sullenly.

'Well, isn't he the lucky one?' Desjardin remarked. 'What are you going to give him for a party favour, Chris, a bloody Kotex? Or how about some used toilet paper? I understand these things seem to be your sack these days.'

Chris went red. 'I'm leaving. I don't have to listen to that.'

Desjardin had not been able to get the image of Carrie out of her mind all weekend, Carrie screaming, blubbering, a wet napkin plastered squarely in the middle of her pubic hair—and her own sick, angry reaction.

And now, as Chris tried to storm out past her, she reached out and slammed her against a row of dented, olive-coloured lockers beside the inner door. Chris's eyes widened with shocked disbelief. Then a kind of insane rage filled her face.

'You can't hit us!' she screamed. 'You'll get canned for this! See if you don't, you *bitch!*'

The other girls winced and sucked breath and stared at the floor. It was getting out of hand. Sue noticed out of the corner of her eye that Fern and Donna Thibodeau were holding hands.

'I don't really care, Hargensen,' Desjardin said. 'If you or any of your girls—think I'm wearing my teacher hat right now, you're making a bad mistake. I just want you all to know that you did a shitty thing on Friday. A really shitty thing.'

Chris Hargensen was sneering at the floor. The rest of the girls were looking miserably at anything but their gym instructor. Sue found herself looking into the shower stall—the scene of the crime—and jerked her glance elsewhere. None of them had ever heard a teacher call anything shitty before.

'Did any of you stop to think that Carrie White has feelings? Do any of you *ever* stop to think? Sue? Fern? Helen? Jessica? Any of you? You think she's ugly. Well, you're all ugly. I saw it on Friday morning.'

Chris Hargensen was mumbling about her father being a lawyer.

"Shut up!" Desjardin yelled in her face. Chris recoiled so suddenly that her head struck the lockers behind her. She began to whine and rub her head.

'One more remark out of you,' Desjardin said softly, 'and I'll throw you across the room. Want to find out if I'm telling the truth?'

Chris, who had apparently decided she was dealing with a mad-woman, said nothing.

Desjardin put her hands on her hips. 'The office has decided on punishment for you girls. Not *my* punishment, I'm sorry to say. My idea was three days' suspension and refusal of your prom tickets.'

Several girls looked at each other and muttered unhappily.

'That would have hit you where you live,' Desjardin continued, 'Unfortunately, Ewen is staffed completely by men in its administration wing. I don't believe they have any real conception of how utterly nasty what you did was. So. One week's detention.'

Spontaneous sighs of relief.

'But. It's to be *my* detention. In the gym. And I'm going to run you ragged.'

'I won't come,' Chris said. Her lips had thinned across her teeth.

'That's up to you, Chris. That's up to all of you. But punishment for skipping detention is going to be three days' suspension and refusal of your prom tickets. Get the picture?'

No one said anything.

'Right. Change up. And think about what I said.'

She left.

Utter silence for a long and stricken moment. Then Chris Hargensen said with loud, hysterical stridency:

'She can't get away with it!' She opened a door at random, pulled out a pair of sneakers and hurled them across the room. 'I'm going to get her! Goddammit! Goddammit! See if I don't! If we all stick together we can—'

'Shut up, Chris,' Sue said, and was shocked to hear a dead, adult lifelessness in her voice. 'Just shut up.'

'This isn't over,' Chris Hargensen said, unzipping her skirt with a rough jab and reaching for her fashionably frayed green gym shorts. 'This isn't over by a long way.'

And she was right.

From *The Shadow Exploded* (pp. 60-61):

In the opinion of this researcher, a great many of the people who have researched the Carrie White matter— either for the scientific journals or for the popular press— have placed a mistaken emphasis on a relatively fruitless search for incidents of telekinesis in the girl's childhood. To strike a rough analogy, this is like spending years researching the early incidents of masturbation in a rapist's childhood.

The spectacular incident of the stones serves as a kind of red herring in this respect. Many researchers have adopted the erroneous belief that where there has been one incident, there must be others. To offer another analogy, this is like dispatching a crew of meteor watchers to Crater National Park because a huge asteroid struck there two million years ago.

To the best of my knowledge, there are no other recorded instances of TK in Carrie's childhood. If Carrie had not been an only child, we might have at least hearsay reports of dozens of other minor occurrences.

In the case of Andrea Kolintz (see Appendix II for a fuller history), we are told that, following a spanking for crawling out on the roof, 'The medicine cabinet flew open, bottles fell to the floor or seemed to hurl themselves across the bathroom, doors flew open and slammed shut, and at the climax of the manifestation, a 300-pound stereo cabinet tipped over and records flew all over the living room, dive-bombing the occupants and shattering against the walls.'

Significantly, this report is from one of Andrea's brothers, as quoted in the September 4, 1955, issue of *Life* magazine. *Life* is hardly the most scholarly or unimpeachable source, but there is a great deal of other documentation, and I think that the point of familiar witnessship is served.

In the case of Carrie White, the only witness to any possible prologue to the final climactic events was Margaret White, and she, of course is dead.

Henry Grayle, principal of Ewen High School, had been expecting him all week, but Chris Hargensen's father didn't show up until Friday—the day after Chris had skipped her detention period with the formidable Miss Desjardin.

'Yes, Miss Fish?' He spoke formally into the intercom, although he could see the man in the outer office through his window, and certainly knew his face from pictures in the local paper.

'John Hargensen to see you, Mr Grayle.'

'Send him in, please.' *Goddammit, Fish, do you have to sound so impressed?*

Grayle was an irrepressible paper-clip-bender, napkin-ripper, corner-folder. For John Hargensen, the town's leading legal light, he was bringing up the heavy ammunition—a whole box of heavy-duty clips in the middle of his desk blotter.

Hargensen was a tall, impressive man with a self-confident way of moving and the kind of sure, mobile features that said this was a man superior at the game of one-step-ahead social interaction.

He was wearing a brown Savile Row suit with subtle glints of green and gold running through the weave that put Grayle's local off-the-rack job to shame. His briefcase was thin, real leather, and bound with glittering stainless steel. The smile was faultless and full of many capped teeth—a smile to make the hearts of lady jurors melt like butter in a warm skillet. His grip was major league all the way—firm, warm, long.

'Mr Grayle, I've wanted to meet you for some time now.'

'I'm always glad to see interested parents,' Grayle said with a dry smile. 'That's why we have Parents Open House every October.'

'Of course.' Hargensen smiled, 'I imagine you're a busy man, and I have to be in court in forty-five minutes from now. Shall we get down to specifics?'

'Surely,' Grayle dipped into his box of clips and began to mangle the first one. 'I suspect you are here concerning the disciplinary action taken against your daughter Christine. You should be informed that school policy on the matter has been set. As a man concerned with the workings of justice yourself, you should realize that bending the rules is hardly possible or—'

Hargensen waved his hand impatiently. 'Apparently you're labouring under a misconception, Mr Grayle. I am

64

here because my daughter was manhandled by your gym teacher, Miss Rhoda Desjardin. And verbally abused, I'm afraid. I believe the term your Miss Desjardin used in connection with my daughter was "shitty." '

Grayle sighed inwardly. 'Miss Desjardin has been reprimanded.'

John Hargensen's smile cooled thirty degrees, 'I'm afraid a reprimand will not be sufficient. I believe this has been the young, ah, lady's first year in a teaching capacity?'

'Yes. We have found her to be eminently satisfactory.'

'Apparently your definition of eminently satisfactory includes throwing students up against lockers and the ability to curse like a sailor?'

Grayle fenced: 'As a lawyer, you must be aware that this state acknowledges the school's title to *in loco parentis*—along with full responsibility, we succeed to full parental rights during school hours. If you're not familiar, I'd advise you to check *Monondock Consolidated School District vs Cranepool or*—'

'I'm familiar with the concept,' Hargensen said. 'I'm also aware that neither the Cranepool case that you administrators are so fond of quoting or the Frick case cover anything remotely concerned with physical or verbal abuse. There is, however, the case of *School District No. 4 vs David*. Are you familiar with it?'

Grayle was. George Kramer, the assistant principal of the consolidated high school in S.D. 14 was a poker buddy. George wasn't playing much poker any more. He was working for an insurance company after taking it upon himself to cut a student's hair. The school district had ultimately paid seven thousand dollars in damages, or about a thousand bucks a snip.

Grayle started on another paper clip.

'Let's not quote cases at each other, Mr Grayle, we're

busy men. I don't want a lot of unpleasantness. I don't want a mess. My daughter is at home, and she will stay there Monday and Tuesday. That will complete her three-day suspension. That's all right.' Another dismissive wave of the hand.

(catch fido good boy here's a nice bone)

'Here's what *I* want,' Hargensen continued. 'One, prom tickets for my daughter. A girl's senior prom is important to her, and Chris is very distressed. Two, no contract renewal of the Desjardin woman. That's for me. I believe that if I cared to take the School Department to court, I could walk out with both her dismissal and a hefty damage settlement in my pocket. But I don't want to be vindictive.'

'So court is the alternative if I don't agree to your demands?'

'I understand that a School Committee hearing would precede that, but only as a formality. But yes, court would be the final result. Nasty for you.'

Another paper clip.

'For physical and verbal abuse, is that correct?'

'Essentially.'

'Mr Hargensen, are you aware that your daughter and about ten of her peers threw sanitary napkins at a girl who was having her first menstrual period? A girl who was under the impression that she was bleeding to death?'

A faint frown creased Hargensen's features, as if someone had spoken in a distant room. 'I hardly think such an allegation is at issue. I am speaking of actions following—'

'Never mind,' Grayle said. 'Never mind what you were speaking of. This girl, Carietta White, was called "a dumb pudding" and was told to "plug it up" and was subjected to various obscene gestures. She has not been in school

66

this week at all. Does that sound like physical and verbal abuse to you? It does to me.'

'I don't intend,' Hargensen said, 'to sit here and listen to a tissue of half-truths or your standard schoolmaster lecture, Mr Grayle, I know my daughter well enough to—'

'Here,' Grayle reached into the wire IN basket beside the blotter and tossed a sheaf of pink cards across the desk, 'I doubt very much if you know the daughter represented in these cards half so well as you think you do. If you did, you might realize that it was about time for a trip to the woodshed. It's time you snubbed her close before she does someone a major damage.'

'You aren't—'

'Ewen, four years,' Grayle overrode him. 'Graduation slated June seventy-nine; next month. Tested I.Q. of a hundred and forty. Eighty-three average. Nonetheless, I see she's been accepted at Oberlin. I'd guess someone—probably you, Mr Hargensen—has been yanking some pretty long strings. Seventy-four assigned detentions. *Twenty* of those have been for harassment of misfit pupils, I might add. Fifth wheels, I understand that Chris's clique calls them Mortimer Snurds. They find it all quite hilarious. She skipped out on fifty-one of those assigned detentions. At Chamberlain Junior High, one suspension for putting a firecracker in a girl's shoe . . . the note on the card says that little prank almost cost a little girl named Irma Swope two toes. The Swope girl has a harelip, I understand. I'm talking about your *daughter*, Mr Hargensen. Does that tell you anything?'

'Yes,' Hargensen said, rising. A thin flush had suffused his features, 'It tells me I'll see you in court. And when I'm done with you, you'll be lucky to get a job selling encyclopedias door to door.'

Grayle also rose, angrily, and the two men faced each other across the desk.

'Let it be court, then,' Grayle said.

He noted a faint flick of surprise on Hargensen's face, crossed his fingers, and went in for what he hoped would be a knockout—or at least a TKO that would save Desjardin's job and take this silk-ass son of a bitch down a notch.

'You apparently haven't realized all the implications of *in loco parentis* in this matter, Mr Hargensen. The same umbrella that covers your daughter also covers Carrie White. And the minute you file for damages on the grounds of physical and verbal abuse, we will cross-file against your daughter on those same grounds for Carrie White.'

Hargensen's mouth dropped open, then closed, 'You can't get away with a cheap gimmick like that, you—'

'Shyster lawyer? Is that the phrase you were looking for?' Grayle smiled grimly. 'I believe you know your way out, Mr Hargensen. The sanctions against your daughter stand. If you care to take the matter further, that is your right.'

Hargensen crossed the room stiffly, paused as if to add something, then left, barely restraining himself from the satisfaction of a hard doorslam.

Grayle blew out breath. It wasn't hard to see where Chris Hergensen came by her self-willed stubbornness.

A. P. Morton entered a minute later. 'How did it go?'

'Time'll tell, Morty,' Grayle said. Grimacing, he looked at the twisted pile of paper clips. 'He was good for seven clips, anyway. That's some kind of record.'

'Is he going to make it a civil matter?'

'Don't know. It rocked him when I said we'd cross-sue.'

'I bet it did.' Morton glanced at the phone on Grayle's desk. 'It's time we let the superintendent in on this bag of garbage, isn't it?'

'Yes,' Grayle said, picking up the phone. 'Thank God my unemployment insurance is paid up.'

'Me too,' Morton said loyally.

From *The Shadow Exploded* (appendix III):

Carrie White passed in the following short verse as a poetry assignment in the seventh grade. Mr Edwin King, who had Carrie for grade seven English, says: 'I don't know why I saved it. She certainly doesn't stick out in my mind as a superior pupil, and this isn't a superior verse. She was very quiet and I can't remember her ever raising her hand even once in class. But something in this seemed to cry out.'

> Jesus watches from the wall.
> But his face is cold as stone.
> And if he loves me—As she tells me
> Why do I feel so all alone?

The border of the paper on which this little verse is written is decorated with a great many cruciform figures which almost seem to dance . . .

Tommy was at baseball practice Monday afternoon, and Sue went down to the Kelly Fruit Company in The Centre to wait for him.

Kelly's was the closest thing to a high school hangout the loosely sprawled community of Chamberlain could boast since Sheriff Doyle had closed the rec centre following a large drug bust. It was run by a morose fat man named Hubert Kelly who dyed his hair black and complained constantly that his electronic pacemaker was on the verge of electrocuting him.

The place was a combination grocery, soda fountain and gas station—there was a rusted Jenny pump out front that Hubie had never bothered to change when the company merged. He also sold beer, cheap wine, dirty books, and a wide selection of obscure cigarettes such as Mirads, King Sano, and Marvel Straights.

The soda fountain was a slab of real marble, and there were four or five booths for kids unlucky enough or friendless enough to have no place to go and get drunk or stoned. An ancient pinball machine that always tilted on the third ball stuttered lights on and off in the back beside the rack of dirty books.

When Sue walked in she saw Chris Hargensen immediately. She was sitting in one of the back booths. Her current amour, Billy Nolan, was looking through the latest issue of *Popular Mechanix* at the magazine rack. Sue didn't know what a rich, Popular girl like Chris saw in Nolan, who was like some strange time traveller from the 1950s with his greased hair, zipper-bejewelled leather jacket, and manifold-bubbling Chevrolet road machine.

'Sue!' Chris hailed, 'come on over!'

Sue nodded and raised a hand, although dislike rose in her throat like a paper snake. Looking at Chris was like looking through a slanted doorway to a place where Carrie White crouched with hands over her head. Predictably she found her own hypocrisy (inherent in the wave and the nod) incomprehensible and sickening. Why couldn't she just cut her dead?

'A dime root beer,' she told Hubie. Hubie had genuine draft root beer, and he served it in huge, frosted 1890s mugs. She had been looking forward to tipping a long one while she read a paper novel and waited for Tommy—in spite of the havoc the root beers raised with her complexion, she was hooked. But she wasn't surprised to find she'd lost her taste for this one.

'How's your heart, Hubie?' she asked.

'You kids,' Hubie said, scraping the head off Sue's beer

70

with a table knife and filling the mug the rest of the way. 'You don't understand nothing. I plugged in my electric razor this morning and got a hundred a ten volts right through this pacemaker. You kids don't know what that's like, am I right?'

'I guess not.'

'No, Christ Jesus forbid you should ever have to find out. How long can my old ticker take it? You kids'll all find out when I buy the farm and those urban renewal poops turn this place into a parking lot. That's a dime.'

She pushed her dime across the marble.

'Fifty million volts right up the old tubes,' Hubie said darkly, and stared down at the small bulge in his breast pocket.

Sue went over and slid carefully into the vacant side of Chris's booth. She was looking exceptionally pretty, her black hair held by a shamrock-green band and a tight basque blouse that accentuated her firm, upthrust breasts.

'How are you, Chris?'

'Bitchin' good,' Chris said a little too blithely. 'You heard the latest? I'm out of the prom. I bet that cocksucker Grayle loses his job, though.'

Sue *had* heard the latest. Along with everyone at Ewen.

'Daddy's suing them,' Chris went on. Over her shoulder; '*Billeee!* Come over here and say hi to Sue.'

He dropped his magazine and sauntered over, thumbs hooked into his side-hitched garrison belt, fingers dangling limply toward the stuffed crotch of his pegged levis. Sue felt a wave of unreality surge over her and fought an urge to put her hands to her face and giggle madly.

'Hi, Suze,' Billy said. He slid in beside Chris and immediately began to massage her shoulder. His face was utterly blank. He might have been testing a cut of beef.

'I think we're going to crash the prom anyway,' Chris

71

said. 'As a protest or something.'

'Is that right?' Sue was frankly startled.

'No,' Chris replied, dismissing it, 'I don't know.' Her face suddenly twisted into an expression of fury, as abrupt and surprising as a tornado funnel. 'That goddamned Carrie White! I wish she'd taken her goddam holy joe routine and stuff it straight up her ass!'

'You'll get over it,' Sue said.

'If only the rest of you had walked out with me . . . Jesus, Sue, why didn't you? We could have had them by the balls. I never figured you for an establishment pawn.'

Sue felt her face grow hot. 'I don't know about anyone else, but I wasn't being anybody's pawn. I took the punishment because I thought I earned it. We did a suck-off thing. End of statement.'

'Bullshit. That fucking Carrie runs around saying everyone but her and her gilt-edged momma are going to hell and you can stick up for her? We should have taken those rags and stuffed them down her throat.'

'Sure. Yeah. See you around, Chris.' She pushed out of the booth.

This time it was Chris who coloured; the blood slammed to her face in a sudden rush, as if a red cloud had passed over some inner sun.

'Aren't you getting to be the Joan of Arc around here! I seem to remember you were in there pitching with the rest of us.'

'Yes,' Sue said trembling. 'But I stopped.'

'Oh, aren't you just *it*?' Chris marvelled. 'Oh my *yes*. Take your root beer with you. I'm afraid I might touch it and turn to gold.'

She didn't take her root beer. She turned and half-walked, half-stumbled out. The upset inside her was very great, too great yet for either tears or anger. She was a get-along girl, and it was the first fight she had been in, physical or verbal, since grade-school pigtail pulling. And it was the first time in her life that she had actively espoused a Principle.

And of course Chris had hit her in just the right place, had hit her exactly where she was most vulnerable: She *was* being a hypocrite, there seemed no way to avoid that, and deeply, sheathed within her and hateful, was the knowledge that one of the reasons she had gone to Miss Desjardin's hour of calisthenics and sweating runs around the gym Floor had nothing to do with nobility. She wasn't going to miss her last Spring Ball for anything. Not for *anything*.

Tommy was nowhere in sight.

She began to walk back toward the school, her stomach churning unhappily, Little Miss Sorority, Suzy Creemcheese, The Nice Girl who only does It with the boy she plans to marry—with the proper Sunday supplement coverage, of course. Two kids. Beat the living shit out of them if they show any signs of honesty; screwing, fighting, or refusing to grin each time some mythic honcho yelled frog.

Spring Ball. Blue gown. Corsage kept all the afternoon in the fridge. Tommy in a white dinner jacket, cummerbund, black pants, black shoes. Parents taking photos posed by the living-room sofa with Kodak Starflashes and Polaroid Big-Shots. Crepe masking the stark gymnasium girders. Two bands: one rock, one mellow. No fifth wheels need apply. Mortimer Snurd, please keep out. Aspiring country club members and future residents of Kleen Korners only.

The tears finally came and she began to run.

From *The Shadow Exploded* (p. 60):

The following excerpt is from a letter to Donna Kellogg

from Christine Hargensen. The Kellogg girl moved from Chamberlain to Providence, Rhode Island, in the fall of 1978. She was apparently one of Chris Hargensen's few close friends and a confidante. The letter is postmarked May 17, 1979:

'So I'm out of the Prom and my yellow-guts father says he won't give them what they deserve. But they're not going to get away with it. I don't know what exactly I'm going to do yet but I guarantee you everyone is going to get a big fucking surprise . . .'

It was the seventeenth. May seventeenth. She crossed the day off the calendar in her room as soon as she slipped into her long white nightgown. She crossed off each day as it passed with a heavy black felt pen, and she supposed it expressed a very bad attitude toward life. She didn't really care. The only thing she really cared about was knowing that Momma was going to make her go back to school tomorrow and she would have to face all of Them.

She sat down in the small Boston rocker (bought and paid for with her own money) beside the window, closed her eyes, and swept Them and all the clutter of her conscious thoughts from her mind. It was like sweeping a floor. Lift the rug of your subconscious mind and sweep all the dirt under. Good-bye.

She opened her eyes. She looked at the hairbrush on her bureau.

Flex.

She was lifting the hairbrush. It was heavy. It was like lifting a barbell with very weak arms. Oh. Grunt.

The hairbrush slid to the edge of the bureau, slid out past the point where gravity should have toppled it, and then dangled, as if on an invisible string. Carrie's eyes had closed to slits. Veins pulsed in her temples. A doctor might have been interested in what her body was doing at that

74

instant; it made no rational sense. Respiration had fallen to sixteen breaths per minute. Blood pressure up to 190/100. Heartbeat up to 140—higher than astronauts under the heavy g-load of lift-off. Temperature down to 94.3°. Her body was burning energy that seemed to be coming from nowhere and seemed to be going nowhere. An electroencephalogram would have shown alpha waves that were no longer waves at all, but great, jagged spikes.

She let the hairbrush down carefully. Good. Last night she had dropped it. Lose all your points, go to jail.

She closed her eyes again and rocked. Physical functions began to revert to the norm; her respiration speeded until she was nearly panting. The rocker had a slight squeak. Wasn't annoying, though. Was soothing. Rock, rock. Clear your mind.

'Carrie?' Her mother's voice, slightly disturbed, floated up.

(she's getting interference like the radio when you turn on the blender good good)

'Have you said your prayers, Carrie?'

'I'm saying them,' she called back.

Yes. She was saying them, all right.

She looked at her small studio bed.

Flex.

Tremendous weight. Huge. Unbearable.

The bed trembled and then the end came up perhaps three inches.

It dropped with a crash. She waited, a small smile playing about her lips, for Momma to call upstairs angrily. She didn't. So Carrie got up, went to her bed, and slid between the cool sheets. Her head ached and she felt giddy, as she always did after these exercise sessions. Her heart was pounding in a fierce, scary way.

She reached over, turned off the light, and lay back. No pillow. Momma didn't allow her a pillow.

She thought of imps and families and witches.

(am i a witch momma the devil's whore)

riding through the night, souring milk, overturning butter churns, blighting crops while They huddled inside their houses with hex signs scrawled on Their doors.

She closed her eyes, slept, and dreamed of huge, living stones crashing through the night, seeking out Momma, seeking out Them. They were trying to run, trying to hide. But the rock would not hide them; the dead tree gave no shelter.

From *My Name is Susan Snell,* by Susan Snell (New York: Simon & Schuster, 1986), pp. i-iv:

There's one thing no one has understood about what happened in Chamberlain on Prom Night. The press hasn't understood it, the scientists at Duke University haven't understood it, David Congress hasn't understood it—although his *The Shadow Exploded* is probably the only half-decent book written on the subject—and certainly The White Commission, which used me as a handy scapegoat, did not understand it.

This one thing is the most fundamental fact: We were kids.

Carrie was seventeen, Chris Hargensen was seventeen, I was seventeen, Tommy Ross was eighteen, Billy Nolan (who spent a year repeating the ninth grade, presumably before he learned how to shoot his cuffs during examinations) was nineteen . . .

Older kids react in more socially acceptable ways than younger kids, but they still have a way of making bad decisions, of over-reacting, or underestimating.

In the first section which follows this introduction I must show these tendencies in myself as well as I am able. Yet the matter which I am going to discuss is at the root of my involvement in Prom Night, and if I am to clear my name, I must begin by recalling scenes which I find particularly painful . . .

I have told this story before, most notoriously before The White Commission, which received it with incredulity. In the wake of two hundred deaths and the destruction of an entire town, it is so easy to forget one thing: We were kids. We were kids. We were kids trying to do our best . . .

'You must be crazy.'

He blinked at her, not willing to believe that he had actually heard it. They were at his house, and the television was on but forgotten. His mother had gone over to visit Mrs Klein across the street. His father was in the cellar workroom making a bird-house.

Sue looked uncomfortable but determined. 'It's the way I want it, Tommy.'

'Well, it's not the way I want it. I think it's the craziest goddam thing I ever heard. Like something you might do on a bet.'

Her face tightened. 'Oh? I thought you were the one making the big speeches the other night. But when it comes to putting your money where your big fat mouth is—'

'Wait, whoa.' He was unoffended, grinning. 'I didn't say no, did I? Not yet, anyway.'

'You—'

'Wait. Just wait. Let me talk. You want me to ask Carrie White to the Spring Ball. Okay, I got that. But there's a couple of things I don't understand.'

'Name them.' She leaned forward.

'First, what good would it do? And second, what makes you think she'd say yes if I asked her?'

'Not say yes! Why—' She floundered. 'You're . . .

everybody likes you and—'

'We both know Carrie's got no reason to care much for people that everybody likes.'

'She'd go with you.'

'Why?'

Pressed, she looked defiant and proud at the same time. 'I've seen the way she looks at you. She's got a crush. Like half the girls at Ewen.'

He rolled his eyes.

'Well, I'm just telling you,' Sue said defensively. 'She won't be able to say no.'

'Suppose I believe you,' he said. 'What about the other thing?'

'You mean what good will it do? Why . . . it'll bring her out of her shell, of course. Make her . . .' She trailed off.

'A part of things? Come on, Suze. You don't believe that bullshit.'

'All right,' she said. 'Maybe I don't. But maybe I still think I've got something to make up for.'

'The shower room?'

'A lot more than that. Maybe if that was all I could let it go, but the mean tricks have been going on ever since grammar school. I wasn't in on many of them, but I was on some. If I'd been in Chris's group, I bet I would have been in on even more. It seemed like . . . oh, a big laugh. Girls can be cat-mean about that sort of thing, and boys don't really understand. The boys would tease Carrie for a little while and then forget, but the girls . . . it went on and on and on and I can't even remember where it started any more. If I were Carrie, I couldn't even face showing myself to the world. I'd just find a big rock and hide under it.'

'You were kids,' he said. 'Kids don't know what they're doing. Kids don't even know their reactions really,

78

actually, hurt other people. They have no, uh, empathy. Dig?'

She found herself struggling to express the thought this called up in her, for it suddenly seemed basic, bulking over the shower-room incident the way sky bulks over mountains.

'But hardly *anybody* ever finds out that their actions really, actually hurt other people! People don't get better, they just get smarter. When you get smarter you don't stop pulling the wings off flies, you just think of better reaons for doing it. Lots of kids say they feel sorry for Carrie White—mostly girls, and *that's* a laugh—but I bet none of them understand what it's like to *be* Carrie White, every second of every day. And they don't really care.'

'Do you?'

'I don't know!' she cried. 'But someone ought to try and be sorry in a way that counts . . . in a way that means something.'

'All right. I'll ask her.'

'You will?' The statement came out in a flat, surprised way. She had not thought he actually would.

'Yes. But I think she'll say no. You've overestimated my box-office appeal. That popularity stuff is bullshit. You've got a bee in your bonnet about that.'

'Thank you,' she said, and it sounded odd, as if she had thanked an Inquisotor for torture.

'I love you,' he said.

She looked at him, startled. It was the first time he had said it.

From *My Name is Susan Snell* (p. 6):

There are lots of people—mostly men—who aren't surprised that I asked Tommy to take Carrie to the Spring Ball. They are surprised that he did it, though, which shows you that the male mind expects very little in the way of altruism from its fellows.

Tommy took her because he loved me and because it was what I wanted. How, asks the sceptic from the balcony, did you know he loved you? Because he told me so, mister. And if you'd known him, that would have been good enough for you, too . . .

He asked her on Thursday, after lunch, and found himself as nervous as a kid going to his first ice-cream party.

She sat four rows over from him in Period Five study hall, and when it was over he cut across to her through the mass of rushing bodies. At the teacher's desk Mr Stephens, a tall man just beginning to run to fat, was folding papers abstractedly back into his ratty brown briefcase.

'Carrie?'

'Ohuh?'

She looked up from her books with a startled wince, as if expecting a blow. The day was overcast and the bank of fluorescents embedded in the ceiling was not particularly kind to her pale complexion. But he saw for the first time (because it was the first time he had really looked) that she was far from repulsive. Her face was round rather than oval, and the eyes were so dark that they seemed to cast shadows beneath them, like bruises. Her hair was darkish blonde, slightly wiry, pulled back in a bun that was not becoming to her. The lips were full, almost lush, the teeth naturally white. Her body, for the most part, was indeterminate. A baggy sweater concealed her breasts except for token nubs. The skirt was colourful but awful all the same: It fell to a 1958 midshin hem in an odd and clumsy A-line. The calves were strong and rounded (the attempt to conceal these with heathery knee-socks was bizarre but unsuccessful) and handsome.

She was looking up with an expression that was slightly fearful, slightly something else. He was quite sure he knew what the something else was. Sue had been right, and being right, he had just time to wonder if this was doing a kindness or making things even worse.

'If you don't have a date for the Ball, would you want to go with me?'

Now she blinked, and as she did so, a strange thing happened. The time it took to happen could have been no more than the doorway to a second, but afterwards he had no trouble recalling it, as one does with dreams or the sensation of *déjà vu*. He felt a dizziness as if his mind was no longer controlling his body—the miserable, out-of-control feeling he associated with drinking too much and then coming to the vomiting point.

Then it was gone.

'What? What?'

She wasn't angry, at least. He had expected a brief gust of rage and then a sweeping retreat. But she wasn't angry; she seemed unable to cope with what he had said at all. They were alone in the study hall now, perfectly between the ebb of old students and the flow of new ones.

'The Spring Ball,' he said, a little shaken. 'It's next Friday and I know this is late notice but—'

'I don't like to be tricked,' she said softly, and lowered her head. She hesitated for just a second and then passed him by. She stopped and turned and he suddenly saw dignity in her, something so natural that he doubted if she was even aware of it. 'Do You People think you can just go on tricking me forever? I know who you go around with.'

'I don't go around with anyone I don't want to,' Tommy said patiently. 'I'm asking you because I want to ask you.' Ultimately, he knew this to be the truth. If Sue was making a gesture of atonement, she was doing it only at secondhand.

The Period Six students were coming in now, and some of them were looking over curiously. Dale Ullman said something to a boy Tommy didn't know and both of them snickered.

'Come on,' Tommy said. They walked out into the hall.

They were halfway to Wing Four—his class was the other way—walking together but perhaps only by accident, when she said, almost too quietly to hear: 'I'd love to. Love to.'

He was perceptive enough to know it was not an acceptance, and again doubt assailed him. Still, it was started. 'Do it, then. It will be all right. For both of us. We'll see to it.'

'No,' she said, and in her sudden pensiveness she could have been mistaken for beautiful. 'It will be a nightmare.'

'I don't have tickets,' he said, as if he hadn't heard. 'This is the last day they sell them.'

'Hey, Tommy, you're going the wrong way!' Brent Gillian yelled.

She stopped. 'You're going to be late.'

'Will you?'

'Your class,' she said distraught. 'Your class. The bell is going to ring.'

'Will you?'

'Yes,' she said with angry helplessness. 'You knew I would.' She swiped at her eyes with the back of her hand.

'No,' he said. 'But now I do. I'll pick you up at seven-thirty.'

'Fine,' she whispered. 'Thank you.' She looked as if she might swoon.

And then, more uncertain than ever, he touched her hand.

From *The Shadow Exploded* (pp. 74-76):

Probably no other aspect of the Carrie White affair has been so misunderstood, second-guessed, and shrouded in mystery as the part played by Thomas Everett Ross, Carrie's ill-starred escort to the Ewen High School Spring Ball.

Morton Cratzchbarken, in an admittedly sensational-ized address to The National Colloquium on Psychic Phenomena last year, said that the two most stunning events of the twentieth century have been the assassin-ation of John F. Kennedy in 1963 and the destruction that came to Chamberlain, Maine, in May of 1979. Cratzchbarken points out that both events were driven home to the citizenry by mass media, and both events have almost shouted the frightening fact that, while something had ended, something else had been irrevo-cably set in motion, for good or ill. If the comparison can be made, then Thomas Ross played the part of Lee Harvey Oswald—trigger man in a catastrophe. The question that still remains is: Did he do so wittingly or unwittingly?

Susan Snell, by her own admission, was to have been escorted by Ross to the annual event. She claims that she suggested Ross take Carrie to make up for her part in the shower-room incident. Those who oppose this story, most lately led by George Jerome of Harvard, claim that this is either a highly romantic distortion or an outright lie. Jerome argues with great force and eloquence that it is hardly typical of high-school-age adolescents to feel that they have to 'atone' for anything—particularly for an offence against a peer who has been ostracized from existing cliques.

'It would be uplifting if we could believe that adolescent human nature is capable of salvaging the pride and self-image of the low bird in the pecking order with such a gesture,' Jerome has said in a recent issue of *The Atlantic Monthly*, 'but we know better. The low bird is not picked tenderly out of the dust by its fellows; rather, it is despatched quickly and without mercy.'

Jerome, of course, is absolutely right—about birds, at any rate—and his eloquence is undoubtedly responsible in large part for the advancement of the 'practical joker' theory, which The White Commission approached but did not actually state. This theory hypothesizes that Ross and Christine Hargensen (see pp. 10-18) were at the centre of a loose conspiracy to get Carrie White to the Spring Ball, and, once there, complete her humiliation. Some theorists (mostly crime writers) also claim that Sue Snell was an active part of this conspiracy. This casts the mysterious Mr Ross in the worst possible light, that of a practical joker deliberately manoeuvring an unstable girl into an situation of extreme stress.

The author doesn't believe that likely in light of Mr Ross's character. This is a facet which has remained largely unexplored by his detractors, who have painted him as a rather dull clique-centred athlete; the phrase 'dumb jock' expresses this view of Tommy Ross perfectly.

It is true that Ross was an athlete of above-average ability. His best sport was baseball, and he was a member of the Ewen varsity squad from his Sophomore year. Dick O'Connell, general manager of the Boston Red Sox, has indicated that Ross would have been offered a fairly large bonus for signing a contract, had he lived.

But Ross was also a straight-A student (hardly fitting the 'dumb-jock' image), and his parents have both said that he had decided pro baseball would have to wait until he had finished college, where he planned to study for an English degree. His interests including writing poetry, and a poem written six months prior to his death was published in an established 'little magazine' called *Everleaf*. This is available in Appendix V.

His surviving classmates also give him high marks, and this is significant. There were only twelve survivors of what has become known in the popular press as Prom Night. Those who were not in attendance were largely the unpopular members of the Junior and Senior classes. If these 'outs' remember Ross as a friendly, good-natured fellow (many referred to him as 'a hell of a good shit'), does not Professor Jerome's thesis suffer accordingly?

Ross's school records—which cannot, according to state law, be photostated here—when taken with classmates' recollections and the comments of relatives, neighbours, and teachers, form a picture of an extraordinary young man. This is a fact that jells very badly with Professor Jerome's picture of a peer-worshipping, sly young tough. He apparently had a high enough tolerance to verbal abuse and enough independence from his peer group to ask Carrie in the first place. In fact, Thomas Ross appears to have been something of a rarity: a socially conscious young man.

No case will be made here for his sainthood. There is none to be made. But intensive research has satisfied me that neither was he a human chicken in a public-school barnyard, joining mindlessly in the ruin of a weaker hen . . .

She lay

(i am not afraid not afraid of her)

on her bed with an arm thrown over her eyes. It was Saturday night. If she was to make the dress she had in mind, she would have to start tomorrow at the

(i'm not afraid momma)

85

latest. She had already bought the material at John's in Westover. The heavy, crumpled velvet richness of it frightened her. The price had also frightened her, and she had been intimidated by the size of the place, the chic ladies wandering here and here in their light spring dresses, examining bolts of cloth. There was an echoing strangeness in the atmosphere and it was worlds from the Chamberlain Woolworth's where she usually bought her material.

She was intimidated but not stopped. Because, if she wanted to, she could send them all screaming into the streets. Mannequins toppling over, light fixtures falling, bolts of cloth shooting through the air in unwinding streamers. Like Samson in the temple, she could rain destruction on their heads if she so desired.

(i am not afraid)

The package was now hidden on a dry shelf in the cellar, and she was going to bring it up. Tonight.

She opened her eyes.

Flex.

The bureau rose into the air, trembled for a moment and then rose until it nearly touched the ceiling. She lowered it. Lifted it. Lowered it. Now the bed, complete with her weight. Up. Down. Up. Down. Just like an elevator.

She was hardly tired at all. Well, a little. Not much. The ability, almost lost two weeks ago, was in full flower. It had progressed at a speed that was—

Well, almost terrifying.

And now, seemingly unbidden—like the knowledge of menstruation—a score of memories had come, as if some mental dam had been knocked down so that strange waters could gush forth. They were cloudy, distorted little-girl memories, but very real for all that. Making the pictures dance on the walls; turning on the water faucets

86

from across the room; Momma asking her

(carrie shut the windows it's going to rain)

to so domething and windows suddenly banging down all over the house; giving Miss Macaferty four flat tyres all at once by unscrewing the valves in the tyres of her Volkswagen; the stones—

(!!!!!!! no no no no no !!!!!!!)

—but now there was no denying the memory, no more than there could be a denying of the monthly flow, and that memory was not cloudy, no, not *that* one; it was harsh and brilliant, like jagged strokes of lightning: the little girl

(momma stop momma can't i can't breathe o my throat o momma i'm sorry i looked momma o my tongue blood in my mouth)

the poor little girl

(screaming: little slut o i know how it is with you i see what has to be done)

the poor little girl lying half in the closet and half out of it, seeing black stars dancing in front of everything, a sweet, faraway buzzing, swollen tongue lolling between her lips, throat circled with a bracelet of puffed, abraded flesh where Momma had throttled her and then Momma coming back, coming for her, Momma holding Daddy Ralph's long butcher knife

(cut it out i have to cut out the evil the nastiness sins of the flesh o i know about that the eyes cut out your eyes)

in her right hand, Momma's face twisted and working, drool on her chin, holding Daddy Ralph's Bible in her other hand

(you'll never look at that naked wickedness again)

and something flexed, not flex but *FLEX,* something huge and unformed and titanic, a wellspring of power that was not hers now and never would be again and then something fell on the roof and Momma screamed and dropped Daddy Ralph's Bible and that was *good*, and then more bumps and thumps and then the house began to throw its furnishings around and Momma dropped the knife and got on her knees and began to pray, holding up her hands and swaying on her knees while chairs whistled down the hall and the beds upstairs fell over and the dining room table tried to jam itself through a window and then momma's eyes growing huge and crazed, bulging, her finger pointing at the little girl

(it's you it's you devilspawn witch imp of the devil it's *you* doing it)

and then the stones and Momma had fainted as their roof cracked and thumped as if with the footfalls of God and then—

Then she had fainted herself. And after that there were no more memories. Momma did not speak of it. The butcher knife was back in its drawer. Momma dressed the huge black and blue bruises on her neck and Carrie thought she could remember asking Momma how she had gotten them and Momma tightening her lips and saying nothing. Little by little it was forgotten. The eye of memory opened only in dreams. The pictures no longer danced on the walls. The windows did not shut themselves. Carrie did not remember a time when things had been different. Not until now.

She lay on her bed, looking at the ceiling, sweating.

'Carrie! Supper!'

'Thank you,

(i am not afraid)

Momma.'

She got up and fixed her hair with a dark-blue headband. Then she went downstairs.

From *The Shadow Exploded* (p. 59):

How apparent was Carrie's 'wild talent' and what did Margaret White, with her extreme Christian ethic, think of it? We shall probably never know. But one is tempted to believe that Mrs White's reaction must have been extreme . . .

'You haven't touched your pie, Carrie.' Momma looked up from the tract she had been perusing while she drank her Constant Comment. 'It's homemade.'

'It makes me have pimples, Momma.'

'Your pimples are the Lord's way of chastising you. Now eat your pie.'

'Momma?'

'Yes?'

Carrie plunged. 'I've been invited to the Spring Ball next Friday by Tommy Ross—'

The tract was forogtten. Momma was staring at her with wide my ears-are-deceiving-me eyes. Her nostrils flared like those of a horse that has heard the dry rattle of a snake.

Carrie tried to swallow an obstruction and only

(i am not afraid o yes i am)

got rid of part of it.

'—and he's a very nice boy. He's promised to stop in and meet you before and—'

'No.'

'—to have me in by eleven. I've—'

'No, no, *no!*'

'—accepted. Momma, please see that I have to start to . . . to try and get along with the world. I'm not like you. I'm funny—I mean, the kids think I'm funny. I don't want to be. I want to try and be a whole person before it's too late to—'

Mrs White threw her tea in Carrie's face.

It was only lukewarm, but it could not have shut off Carrie's words more suddenly if it had been scalding. She sat numbly, the amber fluid dripping from her chin and cheeks on to her white blouse, spreading. It was sticky and smelled like cinnamon.

Mrs White sat trembling, her face frozen except for her nostrils, which continued to flare. Abruptly she threw back her head and screamed at the ceiling.

'God! God! God!' Her jaw snapped brutally over each syllable.

Carrie sat without moving.

Mrs White got up and came around the table. Her hands were hooked into shaking claws. Her face bore a half-mad expression of compassion mixed with hate.

'The closet,' she said. 'Go to your closet and pray.'

'No, Momma.'

'Boys. Yes, boys come next. After the blood the boys come. Like sniffing dogs, grinning and slobbering, trying to find out where that smell is. *That . . . smell!*'

She swung her whole arm into the blow, and the sound of her palm against Carrie's face

(o god i am so afraid now)

was like that flat sound of a leather belt being snapped in air. Carrie remained seated, although her upper body swayed. The mark on her cheek was first white, then blood red.

'The mark,' Mrs White said. Her eyes were large but blank; she was breathing in rapid, snatching gulps of air. She seemed to be talking to herself as the claw hand descended on to Carrie's shoulder and pulled her out of her chair.

'I've seen it, all right. Oh yes. But. I. Never. Did. But for him. He. Took. Me . . .' She paused, her eyes wandering vaguely toward the ceiling. Carrie was terrified. Momma seemed in the throes of some great revelation which might destroy her.

'Momma—'

'In cars. Oh, I know where they take you in their arms. City limits. Roadhouses. Whiskey. Smelling . . . *oh they smell it on you*!' Her voice rose to a scream. Tendons stood out on her neck, and her head twisted in a questing upward rotation.

'Momma, you better stop.'

This seemed to snap her back to some kind of hazy reality. Her lips twitched in a kind of elementary surprise and she halted, as if groping for old bearings in a new world.

'The closet,' she muttered. 'Go to your closet and pray.'

'No.'

Momma raised her hand to strike.

'No!'

The hand stopped in the dead air. Momma stared up at it, as if to confirm that it was still there, and whole.

The pie pan suddenly rose from the trivet on the table and hurled itself across the room to impact beside the living-room door in a splash of blueberry drool.

'I'm going, Momma!'

Momma's overturned teacup rose and flew past her head to shatter above the stove. Momma shrieked and dropped to her knees with her hands over her head.

'Devil's child,' she moaned. 'Devil's child. Satan spawn—'

'Momma, stand up.'

'Lust and licentiousness, the cravings of the flesh—'

'Stand up!'

Momma's voice failed her but she did stand up, with her hands still on her head, like a prisoner of war.

Her lips moved. To Carrie she seemed to be reciting the Lord's Prayer.

'I don't want to fight with you, Momma,' Carrie said, and her voice almost broke from her and dissolved. She struggled to control it. 'I only want to be let to live my own life. I . . . I don't like yours.' She stopped, horrified in spite of herself. The ultimate blasphemy had been spoken, and it was a thousand times worse than the Eff Word.

'Witch,' Momma whispered. 'It says in the Lord's Book: "Thou shalt not suffer a witch to live." Your father did the Lord's work—'

'I don't want to talk about that,' Carrie said. It always disturbed her to hear Momma talk about her father. 'I just want you to understand that things are going to change around here, Momma.' Her eyes gleamed. '*They* better understand it, too.'

But Momma was whispering to herself again.

Unsatisfied, with a feeling of anticlimax in her throat and the dismal rolling of emotional upset in her belly, she went to the cellar to get her dress material.

It was better than the closet. There was that. Anything was better than the closet with its blue light and the overpowering stench of sweat and her own sin. Anything. Everything.

She stood with the wrapped package hugged against her breast and closed her eyes, shutting out the weak glow of the cellar's bare, cobweb-festooned bulb. Tommy Ross didn't love her; she knew that. This was some strange kind of atonement, and she could understand that and respond to it. She had lain cheek and jowl with the concept of penance since she had been old enough to reason.

He had said it would be good—that they would see to it. Well, *she* would see to it. They better not start anything. They just better not. She did not know if her gift had come from the lord of light or of darkness, and now, finally finding that she did not care which, she was overcome with an almost indescribable relief, as if a huge weight, long carried, had slipped from her shoulders.

Upstairs, Momma continued to whisper. It was not the Lord's Prayer. It was the Prayer of Exorcism from Deuteronomy.

From *My Name Is Susan Snell* (p. 23):

They finally even made a movie about it. I saw it last April. When I came out, I was sick. Whenever anything important happens in America, they have to gold-plate it, like baby shoes. That way you can forget it. And forgetting Carrie White may be a bigger mistake than anyone realizes . . .

Monday morning: Principal Grayle and his understudy, Pete Morton, were having coffee in Grayle's office.

'No word from Hargensen yet?' Morty asked. His lips curled into a John Wayne leer that was a little frightened around the edges.

'Not a peep. And Christine has stopped lipping off about how her father is going to send us down the road.' Grayle blew on his coffee with a long face.

'You don't exactly seem to be turning cartwheels.'

'I'm not. Did you know Carrie White is going to the prom?'

Morty blinked. 'With who? The Beak?' The Beak was Freddy Holt, another of Ewen's misfits. He weighed perhaps one hundred pounds soaking wet, and the casual observer might be tempted to believe that sixty of it was nose.

'No,' Grayle said. 'With Tommy Ross.'

Morty swallowed his coffee the wrong way and went into a coughing fit.

'That's the way I felt,' Grayle said.

'What about his girl friend? The little Snell girl?'

'I think she put him up to it,' Grayle said. 'She certainly seemed guilty enough about what happened to Carrie when I talked to her. Now she's on the Decoration Committee, happy as a clam, just as if not going to her Senior prom was nothing at all.'

'Oh,' Morty said wisely.

'And Hargensen—I think he must have talked to some people and discovered we really could sue him on behalf of Carrie White if we wanted to. I think he's cut his losses. It's the daughter that's worrying me.'

'Do you think there's going to be an incident Friday night?'

'I don't know. I do know Chris has got a lot of friends who are going to be there. And she's going around with that Billy Nolan mess; he's got a zooful of friends, too. The kind that make a career out of scaring pregnant ladies. Chris Hargensen has him tied around her finger, from what I've heard.'

'Are you afraid of anything specific?'

Grayle made a restless gesture. 'Specific? No. But I've been in the game long enough to know it's a bad situation. Do you remember the Stadler game in seventy-six?'

Morty nodded. It would take more than the passage of three years to obscure the memory of the Ewen-Stadler game. Bruce Trevor had been a marginal student but a fantastic basketball player. Coach Gaines didn't like him, but Trevor was going to put Ewen in the area tournament for the first time in ten years. He was cut from the team a week before Ewen's last must-win game against the Stadler Bobcats. A regular announced locker inspection had uncovered a kilo of marijuana behind Trevor's civics book. Ewen lost the game—and their shot at the tourney—104-48. But no one remembered that; what they remembered was the riot that had interrupted the game in the fourth period. Led by Bruce Trevor, who righteously claimed he had been bum rapped, it resulted in four hospital admissions. One of them had been the Stadler coach, who had been hit over the head with a first-aid kit.

'I've got that kind of feeling,' Grayle said. 'A hunch. Someone's going to come with rotten apples or something.'

'Maybe you're psychic,' Morty said.

From *The Shadow Exploded* (pp. 92-93):

It is now generally agreed that the TK phenomenon is a geneticrecessive occurrence—but the opposite of a disease like haemophilia, which becomes overt only in males. In that disease, once called 'King's Evil,' the gene is recessive in the female and is carried harmlessly. Male offspring, however, are 'bleeders.' This disease is generated only if an afflicted male marries a woman carrying the recessive gene. If the offspring of such union is male, the result will be a haemophiliac son. If the offspring is female, the result will be a daughter who is a carrier. It should be emphasized that the haemophilia gene *may* be carried recessively in the male as a part of his genetic make-up. But if he marries a woman with the same outlaw gene, the result will be haemophilia if the offspring is male.

In the case of royal families, where intermarriage was common, the chances of the gene reproducing once it entered the family tree were high—thus the name King's Evil. Haemophilia also showed up in significant quantities in Appalachia during the earlier part of this century, and is commonly noticed in those cultures where incest and the marriage of first cousins is common.

With the TK phenomenon, the male appears to be the carrier: the TK gene *may* be recessive in the female, but dominates *only* in the female. It appears that Ralph White carried the gene. Margaret Brigham, by purest chance, also carried the outlaw gene sign, but we may be fairly confident that it was recessive, as no information has ever been found to indicate that she had telekinetic powers resembling her daughter's. Investigations are now being conducted into the life of Margaret Brigham's grandmother, Sadie Cochran—for, if the dominant/recessive pattern obtains with TK as it does with haemophilia, Mrs Cochran must have been TK-dominant.

If the issue of the White marriage had been male, the result would have been another carrier. Chances that the mutation would have died with him would have been excellent, as neither side of the Ralph White-Margaret Brigham alliance had cousins of a comparable age for the theoretical male offspring to marry. And the chances of meeting and marrying another woman with TK gene at random would be small. None of the teams working on the problem have yet isolated the gene.

Surely no one can doubt, in light of the Maine holocaust, that isolating this gene must become one of medicine's number-one priorities. The haemophiliac, or H-gene, produces male issue with a lack of blood platelets. The telekinetic, or TK-gene, produces female Typhoid Marys capable of destroying almost at will . . .

Wednesday afternoon.

Susan and fourteen other students—The Spring Ball Decoration Committee, no less— were working on the huge mural that would hang behind the twin bandstands on Friday night. The theme was Springtime in Venice (who picked these hokey themes, Sue wondered. She had been a student at Ewen for four years, had attended two Balls, and she still didn't know. Why did the goddam thing *need* a theme, anyway? Why not just have a sock hop and be done with it?): George Chizmar, Ewen's most artistic student, had done a small chalk sketch of gondolas on a canal at sunset and a gondolier in a huge straw fedora leaning against the tiller as a gorgeous panoply of pinks and reds and oranges stained both sky and water. It *was* beautiful, no doubt about that. He had redrawn it in silhouette on a huge fourteen-by-twenty-foot canvas flat, numbering the various sections to go with the various chalk hues. Now the Committee was patiently colouring it in, like children crawling over a huge page in a giant's colouring book. Still, Sue thought, looking at her hands and forearms, both heavily dusted with pink chalk, it was going to be the prettiest prom ever.

Next to her, Helen Shyres sat up on her haunches, stretched, and groaned as her back popped. She brushed a hank of hair from her forehead with the back of her hand, leaving a rose-coloured smear.

'*How* in hell did you talk me into this?'

'You want it to be nice, don't you?' Sue mimicked Miss Geer, the spinster chairman (apt enough term for Miss Mustache) of the Decoration Committee.

'Yeah, but why not the refreshment Committee or the Entertainment Committee? Less back, more mind. The mind, that's my area. Besides, you're not even—' She bit down on the words.

'Going?' Susan shrugged and picked up her chalk again. She had a monstrous writer's cramp. 'No, but I still want it to be nice.' She added shyly: 'Tommy's going.'

They worked in silence for a bit, and then Helen stopped again. No one was near them; the closest was Holly Marshall, on the other end of the mural, colouring the gondola's keel.

'Can I ask you about it, Sue?' Helen asked finally. 'God, everybody's talking.'

'Sure.' Sue stopped colouring and flexed her hand.

'Maybe I ought to tell someone, just so the story stays straight. I asked Tommy to take Carrie. I'm hoping it'll bring her out of herself a little . . . knock down some of the barriers. I think I owe her that much.'

'Where does that put the rest of us?' Helen asked without rancour.

Sue shrugged. 'You have to make up your own mind about what we did, Helen. I'm in no position to throw stones. But I don't want people to think I'm uh . . .'

'Playing martyr?'

'Something like that.'

'And Tommy went along with it?' This was the part that most fascinated her.

'Yes,' Sue said, and did not elaborate. After a pause: 'I suppose the other kids think I'm stuck up.'

Helen thought it over. 'Well . . . they're all talking about it. But most of them still think you're okay. Like you said, you make your own decisions. There is, however, a small dissenting faction.' She snickered dolefully.

'The Chris Hargensen people?'

'And the Billy Nolan people. God, he's scuzzy.'

'She doesn't like me much?' Sue said, making it a question.

'Susie, she hates your guts.'

Susan nodded, surprised to find the thought both distressed and excited her.

'I heard her father was going to sue the school department and then he changed his mind,' she said.

Helen shrugged. 'She hasn't made any friends out of this,' she said. 'I don't know what got into us, any of us. It makes me feel like I don't even know my own mind.'

They worked on in silence. Across the room, Don Barrett was putting up an extension ladder preparatory to gilding the overhead steel beams with crepe paper.

'Look,' Helen said. 'There goes Chris now.'

98

Susan looked up just in time to see her walking into the cubby-hole office to the left of the gym entrance. She was wearing wine-coloured velvet hot pants and a silky white blouse—no bra, from the way things were jiggling up front—a dirty old man's dream, Sue thought sourly, and then wondered what Chris could want in where the Prom Committee had set up shop. Of course Tina Blake was on the Committee and the two of them were thicker than thieves.

Stop it, she scolded herself. Do you want her in sackcloth and ashes?

Yes, she admitted. A part of her wanted just that.

'Helen?'

'Hmmmm?'

'Are they going to do something?'

Helen's face took on an unwilling masklike quality. 'I don't know.' The voice was light, over innocent.

'Oh,' Sue said noncommittally.

(you know you know something: accept something goddammit if its only yourself tell me)

They continued to colour, and neither spoke. She knew it wasn't as all right as Helen had said. It couldn't be; she would never be quite the same golden girl again in the eyes of her mates. She had done an ungovernable, dangerous thing—she had broken cover and shown her face.

The late afternoon sunlight, warm as oil and sweet as childhood, slanted through the high, bright gymnasium windows.

From *My Name Is Susan Snell* (p. 40).

I can understand some of what must have led up to the prom. Awful as it was, I can understand how someone like Billy Nolan could go along, for instance. Chris Hargensen led him by the nose—at least, most of the time.

99

His friends were just as easily led by Billy himself. Kenny Garson, who dropped out of high school when he was eighteen, had a tested third-grade reading level. In the clinical sense, Steve Deighan was little more than an idiot. Some of the others had police records; one of them, Jackie Talbot, was first busted at the age of nine, for stealing hubcaps. If you've got a social-worker mentality, you can even regard these people as unfortunate victims.

But what can you say for Chris Hargensen herself?

It seems to me that from first to last, her one and only object in view was the complete and total destruction of Carrie White ...

'I'm not supposed to,' Tina Blake said uneasily. She was a small, pretty girl with a billow of red hair. A pencil was pushed importantly in it. 'And if Norma comes back, she'll spill.'

'She's in the crapper,' Chris said. 'Come on.'

Tina, a little shocked, giggled in spite of herself. Still, she offered token resistance: 'Why do you want to see, anyway? You can't go.'

'Never mind,' Chris said. As always, she seemed to bubble with dark humour.

'Here,' Tina said, and pushed a sheet enclosed in limp plastic across the desk. 'I'm going out for a Coke. If that bitchy Norma Watson comes back and catches you I never saw you.'

'Okay,' Chris murmured, already absorbed in the floor plan. She didn't hear the door close.

George Chizmar had also done the floor plan, so it was perfect. The dance floor was clearly marked. Twin bandstands. The stage where the King and Queen would be crowned

(i'd like to crown that fucking snell bitch carrie too)

at the end of the evening. Ranged along the three sides

of the floor were the prom-goers' tables. Card tables, actually, but covered with a froth of crepe and ribbon, each holding party favours, prom programmes, and ballots for King and Queen.

She ran a lacquered, spade-shaped fingernail down the tables to the right of the dance floor, then the left. There: *Tommy R. & Carrie W.* They were really going through with it. She could hardly believe it. Outrage made her tremble. Did they really think they would be allowed to get away with it? Her lips tautened grimly.

She looked over her shoulder. Norma Watson was still nowhere in sight.

Chris put the seating chart back and rifled quickly through the rest of the papers on the pitted and initial-scarred desk. Invoices (mostly for crepe paper and ha'-penny nails), a list of parents who had loaned card tables, petty-cash vouchers, a bill from Star Printers, who had run off the prom tickets, a sample King and Queen ballot—

Ballot! She snatched it up.

No one was supposed to see the actual King and Queen ballot until Friday, when the whole student body would hear the candidates announced over the school's intercom. The King and Queen would be voted in by those attending the prom, but blank nomination ballots had been circulated to home rooms almost a month earlier. The results were supposed to be top secret.

There was a gaining student move afoot to do away with the King and Queen business all together—some of the girls claimed it was sexist, the boys thought it was just plain stupid and a little embarrassing. Chances were good that this would be the last year the dance would be so formal or traditional.

But for Chris, this was the only year that counted. She stared at the ballot with greedy intensity.

George and Frieda. No way. Frieda Jason was a Jew.

Peter and Myra. No way here, either. Myra was one of the female clique dedicated to erasing the whole horse race. She wouldn't serve even if elected. Besides, she was about as good-looking as the ass end of old drayhorse Ethel.

Frank and Jessica. Quite possible. Frank Grier had made the All New England football team this year, but Jessica was another little sparrowfart with more pimples than brains.

Don and Helen. Forget it. Helen Shyres couldn't get elected dog catcher.

And the last pairing: *Tommy and Sue*. Only Sue, of course, had been crossed out, and Carrie's name had been written in. There was a pairing to conjure with! A kind of strange, shuffling laughter came over her, and she clapped a hand over her mouth to hold it in.

Tina scurried back in. 'Jesus, Chris, you still here? She's *coming*!'

'Don't sweat it, doll,' Chris said, and put the papers back on the desk. She was still grinning as she walked out, pausing to raise a mocking hand to Sue Snell, who was slaving her skinny butt off on that stupid mural.

In the outer hall, she fumbled a dime from her bag, dropped it into the pay phone, and called Billy Nolan.

From *The Shadow Exploded* (pp. 100-101):

One wonders just how much planning went into the ruination of Carrie White—was it a carefully made plan, rehearsed and gone over many times, or just something that happened in a bumbling sort of way?

. . . I favour the latter idea. I suspect that Christine Hargensen was the brains of the affair, but that she herself had only the most nebulous of ideas on how one might 'get' a girl like Carrie. I rather suspect it was she who suggested that William Nolan and his friends make the trip to Irwin Henty's farm in North Chamberlain. The thought of that trip's imagined result would have appealed to a warped sense of poetic justice, I am sure . . .

The car screamed up the rutted Stack End Road in North Chamberlain at a sixty-five that was dangerous to life and limb on the washboard unpaved hardpan. A low-hanging branch, lush with May leaves, occasionally scraped the roof of the '61 Biscayne, which was fender-dented, rusted out, jacked in the back, and equipped with dual glasspack mufflers. One headlight was out; the other flickered in the midnight dark when the car struck a particularly rough bump.

Billy Nolan was at the pink fuzz-covered wheel. Jackie Talbot, Henry Blake, Steve Deighan, and the Garson brothers, Kenny and Lou, were also squeezed in. Three joints were going, passing through the inner dark like the lambent eyes of some rotating Cerberus.

'You sure Henty ain't around?' Henry asked. 'I got no urge to go back up, ole Sweet William. They feed you shit.'

Kenny Garson, who was wrecked to the fifth power, found this unutterably funny and emitted a slipstream of high-pitched giggles.

'He ain't around,' Billy said. Even those few words seemed to slip out grudgingly, against his will. 'Funeral.'

Chris had found this out accidentally. Old man Henty ran one of the few successful independent farms in the Chamberlain area. Unlike the crotchety old farmer with a heart of gold that is one of the staples of pastoral literature, old man Henty was as mean as cat dirt. He did not load his shotgun with rock salt at green-apple time,

103

but with birdshot. He had also prosecuted several fellows for pilferage. One of them had been a friend of these boys, a luckless bastard named Freddy Overlock. Freddy had been caught red-handed in old man Henty's henhouse, and had received a double dose of number-six bird where the good Lord had split him. Good ole Fred had spent four raving, cursing hours on his belly in an Emergency Wing examining room while a jovial interne picked tiny pellets off his butt and dropped them into a steel pan. To add insult to injury, he had been fined two hundred dollars for larceny and trespass. There was no love lost between Irwin Henty and the Chamberlain greaser squad.

'What about Red?' Steve asked.

'He's trying to get into some new waitress at The Cavalier,' Billy said, swinging the wheel and pulling the Biscayne through a juddering racing drift and on to the Henty Road. Red Trelawney was old man Henty's hired hand. He was a heavy drinker and just as handy with the bird-shot as his employer. 'He won't be back until they close up.'

'Hell of a risk for a joke,' Jackie Talbot grumbled.

Billy stiffened. 'You want out?'

'No, uh-uh,' Jackie said hastily. Billy had produced an ounce of good grass to split among the five of them—and besides, it was nine miles back to town. 'It's a *good* joke, Billy.'

Kenny opened the glove compartment, took out an ornate scrolled roach clip (Chris's), and fixed the smouldering butt-end of a joint in it. This operation struck him as highly amusing, and he let out his high-pitched giggle again.

Now they were flashing past No Trespassing signs on either side of the road, barbed wire, newly turned fields. The smell of fresh earth was heavy and gravid and sweet on the warm May air.

Billy popped the headlights off as they breasted the next hill, dropped the gearshift into neutral and killed the ignition. They rolled, a silent hulk of metal, toward the Henty driveway.

Billy negotiated the turn with no trouble, and most of their speed bled away as they breasted another small rise and passed the dark and empty house. Now they could see the huge bulk of barn and beyond it, moonlight glittering dreamily on the cow pond and the apple orchard.

In the pigpen, two sows poked their flat snouts through the bars. In the bar, one cow lowed softly, perhaps in sleep.

Billy stopped the car with the emergency brake—not really necessary since the ignition was off, but it was a nice Commando touch—and they got out.

Lou Garson reached past Kenny and got something out of the glove compartment. Billy and Henry went around to the trunk and opened it.

'The bastard is going to shit where he stands when he comes back and gets a look,' Steve said with soft glee.

'For Freddy,' Henry said, taking the hammer out of the trunk.

Billy said nothing, but of course it was not for Freddy Overlock, who was an asshole. It was for Chris Hargensen, just as everything was for Chris, and had been since the day she swept down from her lofty college-course Olympus and made herself vulnerable to him. He would have done murder for her, and more.

Henry was swinging the nine-pound sledge experimentally in one hand. The heavy block of its business end made a portentous swishing noise in the night air, and the other boys gathered around as Billy opened the lid of the ice chest and took out the two galvanized steel pails. They were numbingly cold to the touch, lightly traced with frost.

105

'Okay,' he said.

The six of them walked quickly to the hogpen, their respiration shortening with excitement. The two sows were both as tame as tabbies, and the old boar lay asleep on his side at the far end. Henry swung the sledge once more through the air, but this time with no conviction. He handed it to Billy.

'I can't,' he said sickly. 'You.'

Billy took it and looked questioningly at Lou, who held the broad butcher knife he had taken from the glove compartment.

'Don't worry,' he said, and touched the ball of his thumb to the honed edge.

'The throat,' Billy reminded.

'I know.'

Kenny was crooning and grinning as he fed the remains of a crumpled bag of potato chips to the pigs. 'Doan worry, piggies, doan worry, big Bill's gonna bash your fuckin heads in and you woan have to worry about the bomb any more.' He scratched their bristly chins, and the pigs grunted and munched contentedly.

'Here it comes,' Billy remarked, and the sledge flashed down.

There was a sound that reminded him of the time he and Henry had dropped a pumpkin off Claridge Road overpass which crossed 495 west of town. One of the sows dropped dead with its tongue protruding, eyes still open, potato chip crumbs around its snout.

Kenny giggled. 'She didn't even have time to burp.'

'Do it quick, Lou,' Billy said.

Kenny's brother slid between the slates, lifted the pig's head toward the moon—the glazing eyes regarded the crescent with rapt blackness—and slashed.

The flow of blood was immediate and startling. Several

of the boys were splattered and jumped back with little cries of disgust.

Billy leaned through and put one of the buckets under the main flow. The pail filled up rapidly, and he set it aside. The second was half full when the flow trickled and died.

'The other one,' he said.

'Jesus, Billy,' Jackie whined. 'Isn't that en—'

'The other one,' Billy repeated.

'Soo-*ee*, pig-pig-pig,' Kenny called, grinning and rattling the empty potato-chop bag. After a pause, the sow returned to the fence, the sledge flashed, the second bucket was filled and the remainder of the blood allowed to flow into the ground. A rank, coppery smell hung on the air. Billy found he was slimed in pig blood to the forearms.

Carrying the pails back to the trunk, his mind made a dim, symbolic connection. Pig blood. That was good. Chris was right. It was really good. It made everything solidify.

Pig blood for a pig.

He nestled the galvanized steel pails into the crushed ice and slammed the lid of the chest. 'Let's go,' he said.

Billy got behind the wheel and released the emergency brake. The five boys got behind, put their shoulders into it, and the car turned in a tight, noiseless circle and trundled up past the barn to the crest of the hill across from Henty's house.

When the car began to roll on its own, they trotted up beside the doors and climbed in, puffing and panting.

The car gained speed enough to slew a little as Billy whipped it out of the long driveway and on to the Henty Road. At the bottom of the hill he dropped the transmission into third and popped the clutch. The engine hitched and grunted into life.

Pig blood for a pig. Yes, that was good, all right. That was really good. He smiled, and Lou Garson felt a start of surprise and fear. He was not sure he could recall ever having seen Billy Nolan smile before. There had not even been rumours.

'Whose funeral did ole man Henty go to?' Steve asked.

'His mother's,' Billy said.

'His *mother*?' Jackie Talbot said, stunned. 'Jesus Christ, she musta been older'n God.'

Kenny's high-pitched cackle drifted back on the redolent darkness that trembled at the edge of summer.

Part Two

Prom Night

She put the dress on for the first time on the morning of May 27, in her room. She had bought a special brassiere to go with it, which gave her breasts the proper uplift (not that they actually needed it) but left their top halves uncovered. Wearing it gave her a weird, dreamy feeling that was half shame and half defiant excitement.

The dress itself was nearly floor-length. The skirt was loose, but the waist was snug, the material rich and unfamiliar against her skin, which was used only to cotton and wool.

The hang of it seemed to be right—or would be, with the new shoes. She slipped them on, adjusted the neckline, and went to the window. She could see only a maddening ghost image of herself, but everything seemed to be right. Maybe later she could—

The door swung open behind her with only a soft snick of the latch, and Carrie turned to look at her mother.

She was dressed for work, wearing her white sweater and holding her black pocketbook in one hand. In the other she was holding Daddy Ralph's Bible.

They looked at each other.

Hardly conscious of it, Carrie felt her back straighten until she stood straight in the patch of early spring sunshine that fell through the window.

'Red,' Momma murmured. 'I might have known it would be red.'

Carrie said nothing.

'I can see your dirtypillows. Everyone will. They'll be looking at your body. The Book says—'

'Those are my breasts, Momma. Every woman has them.'

'Take off that dress,' Momma said.

'No.'

'Take it off, Carrie. We'll go down and burn it in the incinerator together, and then pray for forgiveness. We'll do penance.' Her eyes began to sparkle with the strange disconnected zeal that came over her at events which she considered to be tests of faith. 'I'll stay home from work and you'll stay home from school. We'll pray. We'll ask for a sign. We'll get us down on our knees and ask for the Pentecostal Fire.'

'No, Momma.'

Her mother reached up and pinched her own face. It left a red mark. She looked to Carrie for reaction, saw none, hooked her right hand into claws and ripped it across her own cheek, bringing thin blood. She whined and rocked back on her heels. Her eyes glowed with exultation.

'Stop hurting yourself, Momma. That's not going to make me stop either.'

Momma screamed. She made her right hand a fist and struck herself in the mouth, bringing blood. She dabbled her fingers in it, looked at it dreamily, and daubed a spot on the cover of the Bible.

'Washed in the Blood of the Lamb,' she whispered. 'Many times. Many times he and I—'

'Go away, Momma.'

She looked up at Carrie, her eyes glowing. There was a terrifying expression of righteous anger graven on her face.

'The Lord is not mocked,' she whispered. 'Be sure your sin will find you out. Burn it, Carrie! Cast that devil's red from you and burn it! Burn it! *Burn it!*'

The door slammed open by itself.

'Go away, Momma.'

Momma smiled. Her bloody mouth made the smile grotesque, twisted. 'As Jezebel fell from the tower, let it be with you,' she said. 'And the dogs came and licked up the blood. It's in the Bible! It's—'

Her feet began to slip along the floor and she looked down at them, bewildered. The wood might have turned to ice.

'Stop that!' She screamed.

She was in the hall now. She caught the doorjamb and held on for a moment; then her fingers were torn loose, seemingly by nothing.

'I love you, Momma,' Carrie said steadily. 'I'm sorry.'

She envisioned the door swinging shut, and the door did just that, as if moved by a light breeze. Carefully, so as not to hurt her, she disengaged the mental hands she had pushed her mother with.

A moment later, Margaret was pounding on the door. Carrie held it shut, her lips trembling.

'There's going to be a judgment!' Margaret White raved. 'I wash my hands of it! I tried!'

'Pilate said that,' Carrie murmured.

Her mother went away. A minute later Carrie saw her go down the walk and cross the street on her way to work.

'Momma,' she said softly, and put her forehead on the glass.

From *The Shadow Exploded* (p. 129):

Before turning to a more detailed analysis of Prom Night itself, it might be well to sum up what we know of Carrie White the person.

We know that Carrie was the victim of her mother's religious mania. We know that she possessed a latent telekinetic talent, commonly referred to as TK. We know that this so-called 'wild talent' is really a hereditary trait, produced by a gene that is usually recessive, if present at all. We suspect that the TK ability may be glandular in nature. We know that Carrie produced at least one demonstration of her ability as a small girl when she was put into an extreme situation of guilt and stress. We know that a second extreme situation of guilt and stress arose from a shower-room hazing incident. It has been theorized (especially by William G. Throneberry and Julia Givens, Berkeley) that resurgence of the TK ability at this point was caused by both psychological factors (i.e. the reaction of the other girls and Carrie herself to their first menstrual period) and physiological factors (i.e., the advent of puberty).

And finally, we know that on Prom Night, a third stress situation arose, causing the terrible events which we now must begin to discuss. We will begin with . . .

(i am not nervous not a bit nervous)

Tommy had called earlier with her corsage, and now she was pinning it to the shoulder of her gown herself. There was no momma, of course, to do it for her and make sure it was in the right place, Momma had locked herself in the chapel and had been in there for the last two hours, praying hysterically. Her voice rose and fell in frightening, incoherent cycles.

(i'm sorry momma but I can't be sorry)

When she had it fixed to her satisfaction, she dropped her hands and stood quietly for a moment with her eyes closed.

There was no full-length mirror in the house.

(vanity vanity all is vanity)

but she thought she was all right. She *had* to be. She—

She opened her eyes again. The Black Forest cuckoo clock, bought with Green Stamps, said seven-ten.

114

(he'll be here in twenty minutes)

Would he?

Maybe it was all just an elaborate joke, the final crusher, the ultimate punch line. To leave her sitting here half the night in her crushed-velvet prom gown with its princess waistline, juliet sleeves and simple straight skirt—and her tea roses pinned to her left shoulder.

From the other room, on the rise now; '. . . in hallowed earth! We know thou bring'st the Eye That Watcheth, the hideous three-lobbed eye, and the sound of black trumpets. We most heartily repent—'

Carrie did not think anyone could understand the brute courage it had taken to reconcile herself to this, to leave herself open to whatever fearsome possibilities the night might realize. Being stood up could hardly be the worst of them. In fact, in a kind of sneaking, wishful way she thought it might be for the best if—

(no stop that)

Of course it would be easier to stay here with Momma. Safer. She knew what They thought of Momma. Well, maybe Momma was a fanatic, a freak, but at least she was predictable, the house was predictable. She never came home to laughing, shrieking girls who threw things.

And if he didn't come, if she drew back and gave up? High school would be over in a month. Then what? A creeping, subterranean existence in this house, supported by Momma, watching game shows and soap operas all day on television at Mrs Garrison's house when she had Carrie In To Visit (Mrs Garrison was eighty-six), walking down to the Centre to get a malted after supper at the Kelly Fruit when it was deserted, getting fatter, losing hope, losing even the power to think?

No. Oh dear God, please no.

(please let it be a happy ending)

'—protect us from *he* with the split foot who waits in

115

the alleys and in the parking lots of roadhouses, O Saviour—'

Seven twenty-five.

Restlessly, without thinking she began to lift objects with her mind and put them back down, the way a nervous woman awaiting someone in a restaurant will fold and unfold her napkin. She could dangle half a dozen objects in air at one time, and not a sign of tiredness or headache. She kept waiting for the power to abate, but it remained at high water with no sign of waning. The other night on her way home from school, she had rolled a parked car

(oh please god let it not be a joke)

twenty feet down the main street curb with no strain at all. The courthouse idlers had stared at it as if their eyes would pop out, and of course she stared too, but she was smiling inside.

The cuckoo popped out of the clock and spoke once. Seven-thirty.

She had grown a little wary of the terrific strain using the power seemed to put on her heart and lungs and internal thermostat. She suspected it would be all too possible for her heart to literally burst with the strain. It was like being in another's body and forcing her to run and run and run. You would not pay the cost yourself; the other body would. She was beginning to realize that her power was perhaps not so different from the powers of Indian fakirs, who stroll across hot coals, run needles into their eyes, or blithely bury themselves for periods up to six weeks. Mind over matter in any form is a terrific drain on the body's resources.

Seven thirty-two.

(he's not coming)

(don't think about it a watched pot doesn't boil he'll come)

(no he won't he's out laughing at you with his friends and after a little bit they'll drive by in one of their fast noisy cars laughing and hooting and yelling)

Miserably, she began lifting the sewing machine up and down, swinging it in widening arcs throught the air.

'—and protect us also from rebellious daughters imbued with the willfulness of the Wicked One—'

'Shut up!' Carrie screamed suddenly.

There was startled silence for a moment, and then the babbling chant began again.

Seven thirty-three.

Not coming

(then i'll wreck the house)

The thought came to her naturally and cleanly. First the sewing machine, driven through the living room wall. The couch through a window. Tables, chairs, books and tracts all flying, the plumbing ripped loose and still spurting, like arteries ripped free of flesh. The roof itself, if that were within her power, shingles exploding upward into the night like startled pigeons—

Lights splashed gaudily across the window.

Other cars had gone by, making her heart leap a little, but this one was going much more slowly.

(o)

She ran to the window, unable to restrain herself, and it was him, Tommy, just climbing out of his car, and even under the street light he was handsome and alive and almost . . . crackling. The odd word made her want to giggle.

Momma had stopped praying.

She grabbed her light silken wrap from where it had lain across the back of her chair and put it around her bare shoulders. She bit her lip, touched her hair, and would have sold her soul for a mirror. The buzzer in the hall made its harsh cry.

She made herself wait, controlling the twitch in her hands, for the second buzz. Then she went slowly, with silken swish.

She opened the door and he was there, nearly blinding in white dinner jacket and dark dress pants.

They looked at each other, and neither said a word.

She felt that her heart would break if he uttered so much as the wrong sound, and if he laughed she would die. She felt—actually, physically—her whole miserable life narrow to a point that might be an end or the beginning of a widening beam.

Finally, helpless, she said: 'Do you like me?'

He said: 'You're beautiful.'

She was.

From *The Shadow Exploded* (p. 131):

While those going to the Ewen Spring Ball were gathering at the high school or just leaving pre-Prom buffets, Christine Hargensen and William Nolan had met in a room above a local town-limits tavern called The Cavalier. We know that they had been meeting there for some time; that is in the records of the White Commission. What we don't know is whether their plans were complete and irrevocable or if they went ahead almost on whim . . .

'Is it time yet?' She asked him in the darkness.

He looked at his watch. 'No.'

Faintly, through the board floor, came the thump of the juke playing *She's Got To Be a Saint*, by Ray Price. The Cavalier, Chris reflected, hadn't changed their records since the first time she'd been there with a forged ID two years ago. Of course then she'd been down in the taprooms, not on one of Sam Deveaux's 'specials.'

118

Billy's cigarette winked fitfully in the dark, like the eye of an uneasy demon. She watched it introspectively. She hadn't let him sleep with her until last Monday, when he had promised that he and his greaser friends would help her pull the string on Carrie White if she actually dared to go to the prom with Tommy Ross. But they had been here before, and had had some pretty hot necking sessions— what she thought of as Scotch love and what he would call, in his unfailing ability to pinpoint the vulgar the dry humps.

She had meant to make him wait until he had actually *done* something,

(but of course he did he got the blood)

but it had all begun to slip out of her hands, and it made her uneasy. If she had not given in willingly on Monday, he would have taken her by force.

Billy had not been her first lover, but he was the first she could not dance and dandle at her whim. Before him her boys had been clever marionettes with clear, pimple-free faces and parents with connections and country-club memberships. They drove their own VWs or Javelins or Dodge Chargers. They went to UMass or Boston College. They wore fraternity windbreakers in the fall and muscle-shirts with bright stripes in the summer. They smoked marijuana a great deal and talked about the funny things that happened to them when they were wrecked. They began by treating her with patronizing good fellowship (all high school girls, no matter how good-looking, were Bush League) and always ended up trotting after her with panting, doglike lust. If they trotted long enough and spent enough in the process she usually let them go to bed with her. Quite often she lay passively beneath them, not helping or hindering, until it was over. Later, she achieved her own solitary climax while viewing the incident as a single closed loop of memory.

She had met Billy Nolan following a drug bust at a Cambridge apartment. Four students, including Chris's date for the evening had been busted for possession. Chris and the other girls were charged with being present there. Her father took care of it with quiet efficiency, and asked her if she knew what would happen to his image and his practice if his daughter was taken up on a drug charge. She told him that she doubted if anything could hurt either one, and he took her car away.

Billy offered her a ride home from school one afternoon a week later and she accepted.

He was what the other kids called a white-soxer or a machine-shop Chuck. Yet something about him excited her and now, lying drowsily in this illicit bed (but with an awakening sense of excitement and pleasurable fear), she thought it might have been his car—at least at the start.

It was a million miles from the machine-stamped, anonymous vehicles of her fraternity dates with their ventless windows, fold-up steering wheels, and vaguely unpleasant smell of plastic seat covers and windshield solvent.

Billy's car was old, dark, somehow sinister, the windshield was milky around the edges, as if a cataract was beginning to form. The seats were loose and unanchored. Beer bottles clicked and rolled in the back (her fraternity dates drank Budweiser; Billy and his friends drank Rheingold), and she had to place her feet around a huge, grease-clotted Craftsman toolkit without a lid. The tools inside were of many different makes, and she suspected that many of them were stolen. The car smelled of oil and gas. The sound of straight pipes came loudly and exhilaratingly through the thin floorboards. A row of dials slung under the dash registered amps, oil pressure, and tach (whatever that was). The back wheels were jacked and the hood seemed to point at the road.

120

And of course he drove fast.

On the third ride home one of the bald front tyres blew at sixty miles an hour, the car went into a screaming slide and she shrieked aloud, suddenly positive of her own death. An image of her broken, bloody corpse, thrown against the base of a telephone pole like a pile of rags, flashed through her mind like a tabloid photograph. Billy cursed and whipped the fuzz-covered steering wheel from side to side.

They came to a stop on the left-hand shoulder, and when she got out of the car on knees that threatened to buckle at every step, she saw that they had left a looping trail of scorched rubber for seventy feet.

Billy was already opening the trunk, pulling out a jack and muttering to himself. Not a hair was out of place.

He passed her, a cigarette already dangling from the corner of his mouth. 'Bring that toolkit, babe.'

She was flabbergasted. Her mouth opened and closed twice, like a beached fish, before she could get the words out. 'I—I will not! You almost k—you—almost—you crazy *bastard!* Besides, it's *dirty!*'

He turned around and looked at her, his eyes flat. 'You bring it or I ain't taking you to the fuckin fights tomorrow night.'

'I hate the fights!' She had never been, but her anger and outrage required absolutes. Her fraternity dates took her to rock concerts, which she hated. They always ended up next to someone who hadn't bathed in weeks.

He shrugged, went back to the front end, and began jacking.

She brought the toolkit, getting grease all over a brand-new sweater. He grunted without turning around. His tee-shirt had pulled out of his jeans, and the flesh of his back was smooth, tanned, alive with muscles. It fascinated her, and she felt her tongue creep into the corner of her mouth.

121

She helped him pull the tyre off the wheel, getting her hands black. The car rocked alarmingly on the jack, and the spare was down to the canvas in two places.

When the job was finished and she got back in, there were heavy smears of grease across both the sweater and the expensive red skirt she was wearing.

'If you think—' she began as he got behind the wheel.

He slid across the seat and kissed her, his hands moving heavily on her, from waist to breasts. His breath was redolent of tobacco; there was the smell of Brylcreem and sweat. She broke it at last and stared down at herself, gasping for breath. The sweater was blotted with road grease and dirt now. Twenty-seven-fifty in Jordan Marsh and it was beyond anything but the garbage can. She was intensely, almost painfully excited.

'How are you going to explain that?' he asked, and kissed her again. His mouth felt as if he might be grinning.

'Feel me,' she said in his ear. 'Feel me all over. Get me dirty.'

He did. One nylon split like a gaping mouth. Her skirt, short to begin with, was pushed rudely up to her waist. He groped greedily, with no finesse at all. And something— perhaps that, perhaps the sudden brush with death— brought her to a sudden, jolting orgasm. She had gone to the fights with him.

'Quarter to eight,' he said, and sat up in bed. He put on the lamp and began to dress. His body still fascinated her. She thought of last Monday night, and how it had been. He had—

(no)

Time enough to think of that later, maybe, when it would do something for her besides cause useless arousal. She swung her own legs over the edge of the bed and slid into gossamer panties.

'Maybe it's a bad idea,' she said, not sure if she was testing him or herself. 'Maybe we ought to just get back into bed and—'

'It's a good idea,' he said, and a shadow of humour crossed his face. 'Pig blood for a pig.'

'What?'

'Nothing. Come on. Get dressed.'

She did, and when they left by the back stairs she could feel a large excitement blooming, like a rapacious and night-flowering vine, in her belly.

From *My Name Is Susan Snell* (p. 45):

You know, I'm not as sorry about all of it as people seem to think I should be. Not that they say it right out; *they're* the ones who always say how dreadfully sorry they are. That's usually just before they ask for my autograph. But they expect you to be sorry. They expect you to get weepy, to wear a lot of black, to drink a little too much or take drugs. They say things like: 'Oh, it's such a shame. But you know what happened to her—' and blah, blah, blah.

But sorry is the Kool-Aid of human emotions. It's what you say when you spill a cup of coffee or throw a gutterball when you're bowling with the girls in the league. True sorrow is as rare as true love. I'm not sorry that Tommy is dead any more. He seems too much like a daydream I once had. You probably think that's cruel, but there's been a lot of water under the bridge since Prom Night. And I'm not sorry for my appearance before The White Commission. I told the truth—as much of it as I knew.

But I am sorry for Carrie.

They've forgotten her, you know. They've made her into some kind of a symbol and forgotten that she was a human being, as real as you reading this, with hopes and dreams and blah, blah, blah. Useless to tell you that, I suppose. Nothing can change her back now from something made out of newsprint into a person. But she was, and she hurt. More than any of us probably know, she hurt.

And so I'm sorry and I hope it was good for her, that prom. Until the terror began, I hope it was good and fine and wonderful and magic . . .

Tommy pulled into the parking lot beside the high school's new wing, let the motor idle for just a second, and then switched it off. Carrie sat on her side of the seat, holding her wrap around her bare shoulders. It suddenly seemed to her that she was living in a dream of hidden intentions and had just become aware of the fact. What could she be doing? She had left Momma alone.

'Nervous?' He asked, and she jumped.

'Yes.'

He laughed and got out. She was about to open the door when he opened it for her. 'Don't be nervous,' he said. 'You're like Galatea.'

'Who?'

'Galatea. We read about her in Mr Evers' class. She turned from a drudge into a beautiful woman and nobody even knew her.'

She considered it. 'I want them to know me,' she said finally.

'I don't blame you. Come on.'

George Dawson and Frieda Jason were standing by the Coke machine. Frieda was in an orange tulle concoction, and looked a little like a tuba. Donna Thibodeau was taking tickets at the door along with David Bracken. They were both National Honour Society members, part of Miss Geer's personal Gestapo, amd they wore white slacks and red blazers—the school colours. Tina Blake

124

and Norma Watson were handing out programmes and seating people inside according to their chart. Both of them were dressed in black, and Carrie supposed they thought they were very chic, but to her they looked like cigarette girls in an old gangster movie.

All of them turned to look at Tommy and Carrie when they came in, and for a moment there was a stiff, awkward silence. Carrie felt a strong urge to wet her lips and controlled it. Then George Dawson said:

'Gawd, you look queer, Ross.'

Tommy smiled. 'When did you come out of the tree-tops, Bomba?'

Dawson lurched forward with his fists up, and for a moment Carrie felt stark terror. In her keyed-up state, she came within an ace of picking George up and throwing him across the lobby. Then she realized it was an old game, often played, well-loved.

The two of them sparred in a growing circle. Then George, who had been tagged twice in the ribs, began to gobble and yell: 'Kill them Congs! Get them Gooks! Pongee sticks! Tiger cages!' and Tommy collapsed his guard, laughing.

'Don't let it bother you,' Frieda said, tilting her letter-opener nose and strolling over. 'If they kill each other, I'll dance with you.'

'They look too stupid to kill,' Carrie ventured. 'Like dinosaurs.' And when Frieda grinned, she felt something very old and rusty loosen inside her. A warmth came with it. Relief. Ease.

'Where'd you buy your dress?' Frieda asked. 'I love it.'

'I made it.'

'Made it?' Frieda's eyes opened in unaffected surprise. 'No shit!'

Carrie felt herself blushing furiously. 'Yes I did. I . . . I

125

like to sew. I got the material at John's in Andover. The pattern is really quite easy.'

'Come on,' George said to all of them in general. 'Band's gonna start.' He rolled his eyes and went through a limber, satiric buck-amd-wing. 'Vibes, vibes, vibes. Us Gooks love them big Fender viyyybrations.'

When they went in, George was doing impressions of Flash Bobby Pickett and mugging. Carrie was telling Freida about her dress, and Tommy was grinning, hands stuffed in his pockets. Spoiled the lines of his dinner jacket Sue would be telling him, but fuck it, it seems to be working. So far it was working fine.

He and George and Freida had less than two hours to live.

From *The Shadow Exploded* (p. 132):

The White Commission's stand on the trigger of the whole affair—two buckets of pig blood on a beam over the stage—seems to be overly weak and vacillating, even in light of the scant concrete proof. If one chooses to believe the hearsay evidence of Nolan's immediate circle of friends (and to be brutally frank, they do not seem intelligent enough to lie convincingly), then Nolan took this part of the conspiracy entirely out of Christine Hargensen's hands and acted on his own initiative . . .

He didn't talk when he drove; he liked to drive. The operation gave him a feeling of power that nothing could rival, not even fucking.

The road unrolled before them in photographic blacks and whites, and the speedometer trembled just past seventy. He came from what the social workers called a broken home; his father had taken off after the failure of a badly managed gas-station venture when Billy was twelve, and his mother had four boyfriends at last count. Brucie was in greatest favour right now. He was a Seagram's 7 man. She was turning into one ugly bag, too.

But the car: the car fed him power and glory from its own mystic lines of force. It made him someone to be reckoned with, someone with *mana*. It was not by accident that he had done most of his balling in the back seat. The car was his slave and his god. It gave, and it could take away. Billy had used it to take away many times. On long, sleepless nights when his mother and Brucie were fighting, Billy made popcorn and went out cruising for stray dogs. Some mornings he let the car roll, engine dead, into the garage he had constructed behind the house with its front bumper dripping.

She knew his habits well enough by now and did not bother making conversation that would simply be ignored anyway. She sat beside him with one leg curled under her, gnawing a knuckle. The lights of the cars streaking past them on 302 gleamed softly in her hair, streaking it silver.

He wondered how long she would last. Maybe not long after tonight. Somehow it had all led to this, even the early part, and when it was done the glue that had held them together would be thin and might dissolve, leaving them to wonder how it could have been in the first place. He thought she would start to look less like a goddess and more like the typical society bitch again, and that would make him want to belt her around a little. Or maybe a lot. Rub her nose in it.

They breasted the Brickyard Hill and there was the high school below them, the parking lot filled with plump, glistening daddies' cars. He felt the familiar gorge of disgust and hate rise in his throat. We'll give them something

(a night to remember)

127

all right. We can do that.

The classroom wings were dark and silent and deserted; the lobby was lit with a standard yellow glow, and the bank of glass that was the gymnasium's east side glowed with a soft, orangey light that was ethereal, almost ghostly. Again the bitter taste, and the urge to throw rocks.

'I see the lights, I see the party lights,' he murmured.

'Huh?' She turned to him, startled out of her own thoughts.

'Nothing.' He touched the nape of her neck. 'I think I'm gonna let you pull the string.'

Billy did it by himself, because he knew perfectly well that he could trust nobody else. That had been a hard lesson, much harder than the ones they taught you in school, but he had learned it well. The boys who had gone with him to Henty's place the night before had not even known what he wanted the blood for. They probably suspected Chris was involved, but they could not even be sure of that.

He drove to the school minutes after Thursday night had become Friday morning and cruised by twice to make sure it was deserted and neither of Chamberlain's two police cars was in the area.

He drove into the parking lot with his lights off and swung around in back of the building. Further back, the football field glimmered beneath a thin membrane of ground fog.

He opened the trunk and unlocked the ice chest. The blood had frozen solid, but that was all right. It would have the next twenty-four hours to thaw.

He put the buckets on the ground, then got a number of tools from his kit. He stuck them in his back pocket and grabbed a brown bag from the seat. Screws clinked inside.

He worked without hurry, with the easeful concentration of one who is unable to conceive of interruption. The gym where the dance was to be held was also the school auditorium, and the small row of windows looking toward where he had parked opened on the backstage storage area.

He selected a flat tool with a spatulate end and slid it through the small jointure between the upper and lower panes of one window. It was a good tool. He had made it himself in the Chamberlain metal shop. He wriggled it until the window's slip lock came free. He pushed the window up and slid in.

It was very dark. The predominant odour was of old paint from the Dramatic Club canvas flats. The gaunt shadows of Band Society music stands and instrument cases stood around like sentinels. Mr Downer's piano stood in one corner.

Billy took a small flashlight out of the bag and made his way to the stage and stepped through the red velvet curtains. The gym floor, with its painted basketball lines and highly varnished surface, glimmered at him like an amber lagoon. He shone his light on the apron in front of the curtain. There, in ghostly chalk lines, someone had drawn the floor silhouette of the King and Queen thrones which would be placed the following day. Then the entire apron would be strewn with paper flowers . . . why, Christ only knew.

He craned his neck and shone the beam of his light up into the shadows. Overhead, girders crisscrossed in shadowy lines. The girders over the dance floor had been sheathed in crepe paper, but the area directly over the apron hadn't been decorated. A short draw curtain obscured the girders up there, and they were invisible from the gym Floor. The draw curtain also hid a bank of lights that would highlight the gondola mural.

Billy turned off the flashlight, walked to the left-hand edge of the apron, and mounted a steel-runged ladder bolted to the wall. The contents of his brown bag, which he had tucked into his shirt for safety, jingled with a strange, hollow jolliness in the deserted gymnasium.

At the top of the ladder was a small platform. Now, as he faced outward toward the apron, the stage flies were to his right, the gym itself on his left. In the flies the Dramatic Club props were stored, some of them dating back to the 1920s. A bust of Pallas, used in some ancient dramatic version of Poe's 'The Raven,' stared at Billy with blind, floating eyes from atop a rusting bedspring. Straight ahead, a steel girder ran out over the apron. Lights to be used against the mural were bolted to the bottom of it.

He stepped out on to it and walked effortlessly, without fear, over the drop. He was humming a popular tune under his breath. The beam was inch-thick with dust, and he left long shuffling tracks. Halfway he stopped, dropped to his knees, and peered down.

Yes. With the help of his light he could make out the chalk lines of the apron directly below. He made a soundless whistling.

(bombs away)

He X'd the precise spot in the dust, then beam-walked back to the platform. No one would be up here between now and the Ball; the lights that shone on the mural and on the apron where the King and Queen would be crowned

(they'll get crowned all right)

were controlled from a box backstage. Anyone looking up from directly below would be blinded by those same lights. His arrangements would be noticed only if someone went up into the flies for something. He didn't believe anyone would. It was an acceptable risk.

He opened the brown bag and took out a pair of

Playtex rubber gloves, put them on, and then took out one of two small pulleys he had purchased yesterday. He had gotten them at a hardware store in Boxford, just to be safe. He popped a number of nails into his mouth like cigarettes and got the hammer. Still humming around his mouthful of nails, he fixed the pulley neatly in the corner above the platform. Beside it he fixed a small eyehole screw.

He went back down the ladder, crossed backstage, and climbed another ladder not far from where he had come in. He was in the loft—sort of a catchall school attic. Here there were stacks of old yearbooks, moth-eaten athletic uniforms, and ancient textbooks that had been nibbled by mice.

Looking left, he could shine his light over the stage flies and spotlight the pulley he had just put up. Turning right, cool night air played on his face, from a vent in the wall. Still humming, he took out the second pulley and nailed it up.

He went back down, crawled out the window he had forced, and got the two buckets of pig blood. He had been about his business for a half hour, but it showed no signs of thawing. He picked the buckets up and walked back to the window, silhouetted in the darkness like a farmer coming back from the first milking. He lifted them inside and went in after.

Beam-walking was easier with a bucket in each hand for balance. When he reached his dust-marked X, he put the buckets down, peered at the chalk marks on the apron once more, nodded, and walked back to the platform. He thought about wiping the buckets on his last trip out to them—Kenny's prints would be on them, Don's and Steve's as well—but it was better not to. Maybe they would have a little surprise on Saturday morning. The thought made his lips quirk.

The last item in the bag was a coil of jute twine. He

131

walked back out to the buckets and tied the handles of both with running slipknots. He threaded the screw, then the pulley. He threw the uncoiling twine across to the left, and then threaded that one. He probably would not have been amused to know that, in the gloom of the auditorium, covered and streaked with decades-old dust, grey kitties flying dreamily about his crow's nest hair, he looked like a hunched, half-mad Rube Goldberg intent upon creating the better mousetrap.

He piled the slack twine on top of a stack of crates within reach of the vent. He climbed down for the last time and dusted off his hands. The thing was done.

He looked out the window, then wriggled through and thumped to the ground. He closed the window, reinserted his jimmy, and closed the lock as far as he could. Then he went back to his car.

Chris said chances were good that Tommy Ross and the White bitch would be the ones under the buckets; she had been doing a little quiet promoting among her friends. That would be good, if it happened. But, for Billy, any of the others would be all right too.

He was beginning to think that it would be all right if it was Chris herself.

He drove away.

From *My Name Is Susan Snell* (p. 48):

Carrie went to see Tommy the day before the prom. She was waiting outside one of his classes and he said she looked really wretched, as if she thought he'd yell at her to stop hanging around and stop bugging him.

She said she had to be in by eleven-thirty at the latest, or her momma would be worried. She said she wasn't going to spoil his time or anything, but it wouldn't be fair to worry her momma.

Tommy suggested they stop at the Kelly Fruit after and grab a root beer and a burger. All the other kids would be going to Westover or Lewiston, and they would have the place to themselves. Carrie's face lit up, he said. She told him that would be fine. Just fine.

This is the girl they keep calling a monster. I want you to keep that firmly in mind. The girl who could be satisfied with a hamburger and a dime root beer after her only school dance so her momma wouldn't be worried . . .

The first thing that struck Carrie when they walked in was Glamour. Not glamour but Glamour. Beautiful shadows rustled about in chiffon, lace, silk, satin. The air was redolent with the odour of flowers, the nose was constantly amazed by it. Girls in dresses with low backs, with scooped bodices showing actual cleavage, with Empire waists. Long skirts, pumps. Blinding white dinner jackets, cumberbunds, black shoes that had been spit-shined.

A few people were on the dance floor, not many yet, and in the soft revolving gloom they were wraiths without substance. She did not really want to see them as her classmates. She wanted them to be beautiful strangers.

Tommy's hand was firm on her elbow. 'The mural's nice,' he said.

'Yes,' she agreed faintly.

It had taken on a soft nether light under the orange spots, the boatman leaning with eternal indolence against his tiller while the sunset blazed around him and the buildings conspired together over urban waters. She knew with suddenness and ease that this moment would be with her always, within hand's reach of memory.

She doubted if they all sensed it—they had seen the world—but even George was silent for a minute as they looked, and the scene, the smell, even the sound of the band playing a faintly recognizable movie theme, was locked forever in her, and she was at peace. Her soul knew a moment's calm, as if it had been uncrumpled and smoothed under an iron.

'Viiiiiybes,' George yelled suddenly, and led Frieda out on to the floor. He began to do a sarcastic jitterbug to the old-timey big-band music, and someone catcalled over to him. George blabbered, leered, and went into a brief arms-crossed Cossack routine that nearly landed him on his butt.

Carrie smiled. 'George is funny,' she said.

'Sure he is. He's a good guy. There are lots of good people around. Want to sit down?'

'Yes,' she said gratefully.

He went back to the door and returned with Norma Watson, whose hair had been pulled into a huge, teased explosion for the affair.

'It's on the other SIDE,' she said, and her bright gerbel's eyes picked Carrie up and down, looking for an exposed strap, an eruption of pimples, any news to carry back to the door when her errand was done. 'That's a LOVELY dress, Carrie. Where did you EVER get it?'

Carrie told her while Norma led them around the dance floor to their table. She exuded odours of Avon soap, Woolworth's perfume, and Juicy Fruit gum.

There were two folding chairs at the table (looped and beribboned with the inevitable crepe paper), and the table itself was decked with crepe paper in the school colours. On top was a candle in a wine bottle, a dance programme, a tiny gilded pencil, and two party favours—gondolas filled with Planters Mixed Nuts.

'I can't get OVER it,' Norma was saying. 'You look so DIFFERENT.' She cast an odd, furtive look at Carrie's face and it made her feel nervous. 'You're positively GLOWING. What's your SECRET?'

'I'm Don MacLean's secret lover,' Carrie said. Tommy sniggered and quickly smothered it. Norma's smile slipped a notch, and Carrie was amazed by her own wit—and audacity. That's what you looked like when the joke was on you. As though a bee had stung your rear end. Carrie found she liked Norma to look that way. It was distinctly unchristian.

'Well, I have to get back,' she said. 'Isn't it EXCITING, Tommy?' Her smile was sympathetic: *Wouldn't it be exciting if—?*

'Cold sweat is running down my thighs in rivers,' Tommy said gravely.

Norma left with an odd, puzzled smile. It had not gone the way things were supposed to go. Everyone knew how things were supposed to go with Carrie. Tommy sniggered again.

'Would you like to dance?' he asked.

She didn't know how, but wasn't ready to admit to *that* yet. 'Let's just sit for a minute.'

While he held out her chair, she saw the candle and asked Tommy if he would light it. He did. Their eyes met over its flame. He reached out and took her hand. And the band played on.

From *The Shadow Exploded* (pp. 133-134):

Perhaps a complete study of Carrie's mother will be undertaken someday, when the subject of Carrie herself becomes more academic. I myself might attempt it, if only to gain access to the Brigham family tree. It might be extremely interesting to know what odd occurrences one might come across two or three generations back . . .

And there is, of course, the knowledge that Carrie went home on Prom Night. Why? It is hard to tell just how sane Carrie's motives were by that time. She may have gone for

135

absolution and forgiveness, or she may have gone for the express purpose of committing matricide. In any event, the physical evidence seems to indicate that Margaret White was waiting for her . . .

The house was completely silent.

She was gone.

At night.

Gone.

Margaret White walked slowly from her bedroom into the living room. First had come the flow of blood and the filthy fantasies the Devil sent with it. Then this hellish Power the Devil had given to her. It came at the time of the blood and the time of hair on the body, of course. Oh, she knew the Devil's Power. Her own grandmother had it. She had been able to light the fireplace without even stirring from her rocker by the window. It made her eyes glow with

(thou shalt not suffer a witch to live)

a kind of witch's light. And sometimes, at the supper table the sugar bowl would whirl madly like a dervish. Whenever it happened, Gram would cackle crazily and drool and make the sign of the Evil Eye all around her. Sometimes she panted like a dog on a hot day, and when she died of a heart attack at sixty-six, senile to the point of idiocy even at that early age, Carrie had not even been a year old. Margaret had gone into her bedroom not four weeks after Gram's funeral and there her girl-child had lain in her crib, laughing and gurgling, watching a bottle that was dangling in thin air over her head.

Margaret had almost killed her then. Ralph had stopped her.

She should not have let him stop her.

Now Margaret White stood in the middle of the living

room. Christ on Calvary looked down at her with his wounded, suffering, reproachful eyes. The Black Forest cuckoo clock ticked. It was ten minutes after eight.

She had been able to feel, actually *feel* the Devil's Power working in Carrie. It crawled all over you, lifting and pulling like evil, tickling little fingers. She had set out to do her duty again when Carrie was three, when she had caught her looking in sin at the Devil's slut in the next yard over. Then the stones had come, and she had weakened. And the power had risen again, after thirteen years. God was not mocked.

First the blood, then the power,

(you sign your name you sign it in blood)

now a boy and dancing and he would take her to a roadhouse after, take her into the parking lot, take her into the back seat, take her—

Blood, fresh blood. Blood was always at the root of it, and only blood could expiate it.

She was a big woman with massive upper arms that had swarfed her elbows to dimples, but her head was surprisingly small on the end of her strong, corded neck. It had once been a beautiful face. It was still beautiful in a weird, zealous way. But the eyes had taken on a strange, wandering cast, and the lines had deepened cruelly around the denying but oddly weak mouth. Her hair, which had been almost all black a year ago, was now almost white.

The only way to kill sin, true black sin, was to drown it in the blood of

(she must be sacrificed)

a repentant heart. Surely God understood that, and had laid His finger upon her. Had not God Himself commanded Abraham to take his son Isaac up upon the mountain?

She shuffled out into the kitchen in her old and splayed

137

slippers, and opened the kitchen utensil drawer. The knife they used for carving was long and sharp and arched in the middle from constant honing. She sat down on the high stool by the counter, found the sliver of whetstone in its small aluminium dish, and began to scrub it along the gleaming edge of the blade with the apathetic, fixated attention of the damned.

The Black Forest cuckoo clock ticked and ticked and finally the bird jumped out to call once and announce eight-thirty.

In her mouth she tasted olives.

THE SENIOR CLASS PRESENTS SPRING BALL '79

May 27, 1979

Music by The Billy Bosman Band
Music by Josie and the Moonglows

ENTERTAINMENT

'Cabaret'—Baton Twirling by Sandra Stenchfield
'500 Miles'
'Lemon Tree'
'Mr Tambourine Man'
    Folk Music by John Swithen and Maureen Cowan
'The Street Where You Live'
'Raindrops Keep Fallin' on My Head'
    Ewen High School Chorus
'Bridge Over Troubled Waters'

CHAPERONES

Mr Stephens, Miss Geer, Mr and Mrs Lublin, Miss Desjardin
   Coronation at 10:00 P.M.
   Remember, it's YOUR prom; make it one to remember always!

When he asked her the third time, Carrie had to admit that she didn't know how to dance. She didn't add that, now that the rock band had taken over for a half-hour set, she would feel out of place gyrating on the floor.

(and sinful)

yes, and sinful.

Tommy nodded, then smiled. He leaned forward and told her that he hated to dance. Would she like to go around and visit some of the other tables? Trepidation rose thickly in her throat, but she nodded. Yes, that would be nice. He was seeing to her. She must see to him (even if he really did not expect it); that was part of the deal. And she felt dusted over with the enchantment of the evening. She was suddenly hopeful that no one would stick out a foot or slyly paste a kick-me-hard sign on her back or suddenly squirt water in her face from a novelty carnation and retreat cackling while everyone laughed and pointed and catcalled.

And if there was enchantment, it was not divine but pagan.

'Carrie?' a voice said hesitantly.

She had been so wrapped up in watching the band and the dance floor and the other tables that she hadn't seen anyone coming at all. Tommy had gone to get them punch.

She turned around and saw Miss Desjardin.

For a moment the two of them merely looked at each other, and the memory travelled between them, communicated

(she saw me she saw me naked and screaming and bloody)

without words or thought. It was in the eyes.

Then Carrie said shyly: 'You look very pretty, Miss Desjardin.'

She did. She was dressed in a glimmering silver sheath, a perfect complement to her blonde hair, which was up. A simple pendant hung around her neck. She looked very young, young enough to be attending rather than chaperoning.

'Thank you.' She hesitated, then put a gloved hand on Carrie's arm. 'You are beautiful,' she said, and each word carried a peculiar emphasis.

Carrie felt herself blushing again and dropped her eyes to the table. 'It's awfully nice of you to say so. I know I'm not . . . not really . . . but thank you anyway.'

'It's true,' Desjardin said. 'Carrie, anything that happened before . . . well, it's all forgotten. I wanted you to know that.'

'I can't forget it,' Carrie said. She looked up. The words that rose to her lips were: *I don't blame anyone any more.* She bit them off. It was a lie. She blamed them all and always would, and she wanted more than anything else to be honest. 'But it's over with. Now it's over with.'

Miss Desjardin smiled, and her eyes seemed to catch and hold the soft mix of lights in an almost liquid sparkling. She looked across toward the dance floor, and Carrie followed her gaze.

'I remember my own prom,' Desjardin said softly. 'I was two inches taller than the boy I went with when I was in my heels. He gave me a corsage that clashed with my gown. The tailpipe was broken on his car and

140

the engine made . . . oh, an awful racket. But it was magic, I don't know why. But I've never had a date like it, ever again.' She looked at Carrie. 'Is it like that for you?'

'It's very nice,' Carrie said.

'And is that all?'

'No. There's more. I couldn't tell it all. Not to anybody.'

Desjardin smiled and squeezed her arm. 'You'll never forget it,' she said. 'Never.'

'I think you're right.'

'Have a lovely time, Carrie.'

'Thank you.'

Tommy came up with two Dixie cups of punch as Desjardin left, walking around the dance floor toward the chaperones' table.

'What did she want?' he asked, putting the Dixie cups down carefully.

Carrie, looking after her, said: 'I think she wanted to say she was sorry.'

(momma untie your apron strings i'm getting big)

and she wanted it that way.

'Look,' he said as they got up.

Two or three stagehands were sliding the King and Queen thrones from the wings while Mr Lavoie, the head custodian, directed them with hand motions toward preset marks on the apron. She thought they looked quite Arthurian, those thrones, dressed all in blinding white, strewn with real flowers as well as huge crepe banners.

'They're beautiful,' she said.

'*You're* beautiful,' Tommy said, and she became quite sure that nothing bad could happen this night—perhaps they themselves might even be voted King and Queen of the Prom. She smiled at her own folly.

141

It was nine o'clock.

Sue Snell sat quietly in the living room of her house, hemming a dress and listening to the Jefferson Airplane *Long John Silver* album. It was old and badly scratched, but soothing.

Her mother and father had gone out for the evening. They knew what was going on, she was sure of that, but they had spared her the bumbling talks about how proud they were of Their Girl, or how glad they were that she was finally Growing Up. She was glad they had decided to leave her alone, because she was still uncomfortable about her own motives and afraid to examine them too deeply, lest she discover a jewel of selfishness glowing and winking at her from the black velvet of her subconscious.

She had done it; that was enough; she was satisfied.

(maybe he'll fall in love with her)

She looked up as if someone had spoken from the hallway, a startled smile curving her lips. That would be a fairy-tale ending, all right. The Prince bends over the Sleeping Beauty, touches his lips to hers.

Sue, I don't know how to tell you this but—

The smile faded.

Her period was late. Almost a week late. And she had always been as regular as an almanac.

The record changer clicked; another record dropped down. In the sudden, brief silence, she heard something within her turn over. Perhaps only her soul.

It was nine-fifteen.

Billy drove to the far end of the parking lot and pulled into a stall that faced the asphalt ramp leading to the highway. Chris started to get out and he jerked her back. His eyes glowed ferally in the dark.

'What?' she said with angry nervousness.

'They use a P.A. system to announce the King and

Queen,' he said. 'Then one of the bands will play the school song. That means they're sitting there in those thrones, on target.'

'I know all that. Let go of me. You're hurting.'

He squeezed her wrist tighter still and felt small bones grind. It gave him a grim pleasure. Still, she didn't cry out. She was pretty good.

'You listen to me. I want you to know what you're getting into. Pull the rope when the song is playing. Pull it hard. There will be a little slack between the pulleys, but not much. When you pull it and feel those buckets go, *run*. You don't stick around to hear the screams or anything else. This is out of the cute-little-joke league. This is criminal assault, you know? They don't fine you. They put you in jail and throw the key over their shoulder.'

It was an enormous speech for him.

Her eyes only glared at him, full of defiant anger.

'Dig it?'

'Yes.'

'All right. When the buckets go, I'm going to run. When I get to the car, I'm going to drive away. If you're there, you can come. If you're not, I'll leave you. If I leave you and you spill your guts, I'll kill you. Do you believe me?'

'Yes. Take your fucking hand off me.'

He did. An unwilling shadow-grin touched his face. 'Okay. It's going to be good.'

They got out of the car.

It was almost nine-thirty.

Vic Mooney, President of the Senior Class, was calling jovially into the mike: 'All right, ladies and gennelmen. Take your seats, please. It's time for the voting. We're going to vote for the King and Queen.'

'This contest insults women!' Myra Crewes called with uneasy good nature.

143

'It insults men, too!' George Dawson called back, and there was general laughter. Myra was silent. She had made her token protest.

'Take your seats, please!' Vic was smiling into the mike, smiling and blushing furiously, fingering a pimple on his chin. The huge Venetian boatman behind him looked dreamily over Vic's shoulder. 'Time to vote.'

Carrie and Tommy sat down. Tina Blake and Norma Watson were circulating mimeographed ballots, and when Norma dropped one at their table and breathed 'Good LUCK!' Carrie picked up the ballot and studied it. Her mouth popped open.

'Tommy, we're *on* here!'

'Yeah, I saw that,' he said. 'The school votes for single candidates and their dates get sort of shanghaied into it. Welcome aboard. Shall we decline?'

She bit her lip and looked at him. 'Do you want to decline?'

'Hell, no,' he said cheerfully. 'If you win, all you do is sit up there for the school song and one dance and wave a sceptre and look like a goddam idiot. They take your picture for the yearbook so everyone can see you look like a goddam idiot.'

'Who do we vote for?' She looked doubtfully from the ballot to the tiny pencil by her boatful of nuts. 'They're more your crowd than mine.' A chuckle escaped her. 'In fact, I don't really have a crowd.'

He shrugged. 'Let's vote for ourselves. To the devil with false modesty.'

She laughed out loud, then clapped a hand over her mouth. The sound was almost entirely foreign to her. Before she could think, she circled their names, third from the top. The tiny pencil broke in her hand, and she gasped. A splinter had scratched the pad of one finger, and a small bead of blood welled.

'You hurt yourself?'

'No.' She smiled, but suddenly it was difficult to smile. The sight of the blood was distasteful to her. She blotted it away with her napkin. 'But I broke the pencil and it was a souvenir. Stupid me.'

'There's your boat,' he said, and pushed it toward her. 'Toot, toot.' Her throat closed, and she felt sure she would weep and then be ashamed. She did not, but her eyes glimmered like prisms and she lowered her head so he would not see.

The band was playing catchy fill-in music while the Honour Society ushers collected the folded-over ballots. They were taken to the chaperones' table by the door, where Vic and Mr Stephens and the Lublins counted them. Miss Geer surveyed it all with grim gimlet eyes.

Carrie felt an unwilling tension worm into her, tightening muscles in her stomach and back. She held Tommy's hand tightly. It was absurd, of course. No one was going to vote for them. The stallion, perhaps, but not when harnessed in tandem with a she-ox. It would be Frank and Jessica or maybe Don Farnham and Helen Shyres. Or—hell!

Two piles were growing larger than the others. Mr Stephens finished dividing the slips and all four of them took turns at counting the large piles, which looked about the same. They put their heads together, conferred, and counted once more. Mr Stephens nodded, thumbed the ballots once more like a man about to deal a hand of poker, and gave them back to Vic. He climbed back on stage and approached the mike. The Billy Bosman Band played a flourish. Vic smiled nervously, harrumphed into the mike, and blinked at the sudden feedback whine. He nearly dropped the ballots to the floor, which was covered with heavy electrical cables, and somebody snickered.

'We've sort of hit a snag,' Vic said artlessly. 'Mr Lublin

says this is the first time in the history of the Spring Ball—'

'How far does he go back?' someone behind Tommy grumbled. 'Eighteen hundred?'

'We've got a tie.'

This got a murmer from the crowd. 'Polka dots or striped?' George Dawson called, and there was some laughter. Vic gave a twitchy smile and almost dropped the ballots again.

'Sixty-three votes for Frank Grier and Jessica MacLean, and sixty-three votes for Thomas Ross and Carrie White.'

This was followed by a moment of silence, and then sudden, swelling applause. Tommy looked across at his date. Her head was lowered, as if in shame, but he had a sudden feeling.

(carrie carrie carrie)

not unlike the one he had had when he asked her to the prom. His mind felt as if something alien was moving in there, calling Carrie's name over and over again. As if—

'Attention!' Vic was calling. 'If I could have your attention, please.' The applause quieted. 'We're going to have a run-off ballot. When the people passing out the slips of paper get to you, please write the couple you favour on it.'

He left the mike, looking relieved.

The ballots were circulated; they had been hastily torn from leftover prom programmes. The band played unnoticed and people talked excitedly.

'They weren't applauding for us,' Carrie said, looking up. The thing he had felt (or thought he had felt) was gone. 'It couldn't have been for us.'

'Maybe it was for you.'

She looked at him, mute.

*

146

'What's taking it so long?' she hissed at him. 'I heard them clap. Maybe that was it. If you fucked up—' The length of jute cord hung between them limply, untouched since Billy had poked a screwdriver through the vent and lifted it out.

'Don't worry,' he said calmly. 'They'll play the school song. They always do.'

'But—'

'Shut up. You talk too fucking much.' The tip of his cigarette winked peacefully in the dark.

She shut. But

(oh when this is over you're going to get it buddy maybe you'll go to bed with lover's nuts tonight)

her mind ran furiously over his words, storing them. People did not speak to her in such a manner. Her father was a lawyer.

It was seven minutes to ten.

He was holding the broken pencil in his hand, ready to write, when she touched his wrist lightly, tentatively.

'Don't . . .'

'What?'

'Don't vote for us,' she said finally.

He raised his eyebrows quizzically. 'Why not? In for a penny, in for a pound. That's what my mother always says.'

(mother)

A picture rose in her mind instantly, her mother droning endless prayers to a towering, faceless, columnar God who prowled roadhouse parking lots with a sword of fire in one hand. Terror rose in her blackly, and she had to fight with all her spirit to hold it back. She could not explain her dread, her sense of premonition. She could only smile helplessly and repeat: 'Don't. Please.'

The Honour Society ushers were coming back, collect-

147

ing folded slips. He hesitated a moment longer, then suddenly scrawled *Tommy and Carrie* on the ragged slip of paper. 'For you,' he said. 'Tonight you go first-class.'

She could not reply, for the premonition was on her: her mother's face.

The knife slipped from the whetstone, and in an instant it had sliced the cup of her palm below the thumb.

She looked at the cut. It bled slowly, thickly, from the open lips of the wound running out of her hand and spotting the worn linoleum of the kitchen floor. Good, then. It was good. The blade had tasted flesh and let blood. She did not bandage it but tipped the flow over the cutting edge, letting the blood dull the blade's sharp glimmer, then she began to sharpen again, heedless of the droplets which splattered her dress.

If thine right eye offend thee, pluck it out

If it was a hard scripture, it was also sweet and good. A fitting scripture for those who lurked in the doorway shadows of onenight hotels and in the weeds behind bowling alleys.

Pluck it out

(oh and the nasty music they play)

Pluck it

(the girls show their underwear how it sweats how it sweats blood)

ou!

The Black Forest cuckoo began to strike ten *and*

(cut her guts out on the floor)

if thine right eye offend thee, pluck it out

The dress was done and she could not watch the television or take out her books or call Nancy on the phone. There was nothing to do but sit on the sofa facing the blackness of the kitchen window and feel some nameless sort of fear

148

growing in her like an infant coming to dreadful term.

With a sigh she began to massage her arms absently. They were cold and prickly. It was twelve after ten and there was no reason, really no reason, to feel that the world was coming to an end.

The stacks were higher this time, but they still looked exactly the same. Again, three counts were taken to make sure. Then Vic Mooney went to the mike again. He paused a moment, relishing the blue feel of tension in the air, and then announced simply:

'Tommy and Carrie win. By one vote.'

Dead silence for a moment, then applause filled the hall again, some of it not without satiric overtones. Carrie drew in a startled, smothered gasp, and Tommy again felt (but for only a second) that weird vertigo in his mind

(carrie carrie carrie carrie)

that seemed to blank out all thought but the name and image of this strange girl he was with. For a fleeting second he was literally scared shitless.

Something fell on the floor with a clink, and at the same instant the candle between them whiffed out.

Then Josie and the Moonglows were playing a rock version of *Pomp and Circumstance*, the ushers appeared at their table (almost magically; all this had been rehearsed meticulously by Miss Geer who, according to rumour, ate slow and clumsy ushers for lunch), a sceptre wrapped in aluminium foil was thrust into Tommy's hand, a robe with a lush dog-fur collar was thrown over Carrie's shoulders, and they were being led down the centre aisle by a boy and a girl in white blazers. The band blared. The audience applauded. Miss Geer looked vindicated. Tommy Ross was grinning bemusedly.

They were ushered up the steps to the apron, led across to the thrones, and seated. Still the applause swelled. The sarcasm in it was lost now; it was honest and deep, a little frightening. Carrie was glad to sit down. It was all happening too fast. Her legs were trembling under her and suddenly, even with the comparatively high neck of her gown, her breasts

(dirtypillows)

felt dreadfully exposed. The sound of the applause in her ears made her feel woozy, amost punch-drunk. Part of her was actually convinced that all this was a dream from which she would wake with mixed feelings of loss and relief.

Vic boomed into the mike: 'The King and Queen of the 1979 Spring Ball—Tommy ROSS and Carrie WHITE!'

Still applause, swelling and booming and crackling. Tommy Ross in the fading moments of his life now, took Carrie's hand and grinned at her, thinking that Suzie's intuition had been very right. Somehow she grinned back. Tommy

(she was right and i love her well i love this one too this carrie she is beautiful and it's right and i love all of them the light the light in her eyes)

and Carrie

(can't see them the lights are too bright i can hear them but can't see them the shower remember the shower o momma it's too high i think i want to get down o are they laughing and ready to throw things to point and scream with laughter i can't see them i can't see them it's all too bright)

and the beam above them.

Both bands, in a sudden and serendipitous coalition of rock and brass, swung into the school song. The audience rose to its feet and began to sing, still applauding.

It was ten-o-seven.

Billy had just flexed his knees to make the joints pop. Chris Hargensen stood next to him with increasing signs of nervousness. Her hands played aimlessly along the seams of the jeans she had worn and she was biting the softness of her lower lip, chewing at it, making it a little ragged.

'You think they'll vote for *them*?, Billy said softly.

'They will,' she said. 'I set it up. It won't even be close. Why do they keep applauding? What's going on in there?'

'Don't ask me, babe. I—'

The school song suddenly roared out, full and strong on the soft May air, and Chris jumped as if stung. A soft gasp of surprise escaped her.

All rise for Thomas Ewen Hiiiiyyygh . . .

'Go on,' he said. 'They're there.' His eyes glowed softly in the dark. The odd half-grin had touched his features.

She licked her lips. They both stared at the length of jute cord.

We'll raise your banners to the skyyyyy

'Shut up,' she whispered. She was trembling, and he thought that her body had never looked so lush or exciting. When this was over he was going to have her until every other time she'd been had was like two pumps with a fag's little finger. He was going on her like a raw cob through butter.

'No guts, babe?'

He leaned forward. 'I won't pull it for you, babe. It can sit there till hell freezes.'

With pride we wear the red and whiiyyyte

A sudden smothered sound that might have been a half-scream came from her mouth, and she leaned forward and pulled violently on the cord with both hands. It came loose with slack for a moment, making her think that Billy had been having her on all this time, that the rope was attached to nothing but thin air. Then it snubbed tight, held for a second, and then came through her palms harshly, leaving a thin burn.

'I—' she began.

The music inside came to a jangling, discordant halt. For a moment ragged voices continued oblivious, and then they stopped. There was a beat of silence, and then someone screamed. Silence again.

They stared at each other in the dark, frozen by the actual act as thought never could have done. Her very breath turned to glass in her throat.

Then, inside, the laughter began.

It was ten twenty-five, and the feeling had been getting worse and worse. Sue stood in front of the gas range on one foot, waiting for the milk to begin steaming so she could dump in the Nestle's. Twice she had begun to go upstairs and put on a nightgown and twice she had stopped, drawn for no reason at all to the kitchen window that looked down Brickyard Hill and the spiral of Route 6 that led into town.

Now, as the whistle mounted atop the town hall on Main Street suddenly began to shriek into the night, rising and falling in cycles of panic, she did not even turn immediately to the window, but only turned the heat off under the milk so it would not burn.

The town hall whistle went off every day at twelve noon and that was all, except to call the volunteer fire department during grass-fire season in August and September. It was strictly for major disasters and its sound was dreamy and terrifying in the empty house.

She went to the window, but slowly. The shrieking of the whistle rose and fell, rose and fell. Somewhere, horns were beginning to blast, as if for a wedding. She could see her reflection in the darkened glass, lips parted, eyes wide, and then the condensation of her breath obscured it.

A memory, half-forgotten, came to her. As children in

152

grammar school, they had practised air-raid drills. When the teacher clapped her hands and said, 'The town whistle is blowing,' you were supposed to crawl under your desk and put your hands over your head and wait, either for the all-clear or for enemy missiles to blow you to powder. Now, in her mind, as clearly as a leaf pressed in plastic,

(the town whistle is blowing)

she heard the words clang in her mind.

Far below, to the left, where the high school parking lot was—the ring of sodium arc lamps made it a sure landmark, although the school building itself was invisible in the dark—a spark glowed as if God has struck a flint-and-steel.

(that's where the oil tanks are)

The spark hesitated, then bloomed orange. Now you could see the school, and it was on fire.

She was already on her way to the closet to get her coat when the first dull, booming explosion shook the floor under her feet and made her mother's china rattle in the cupboards.

From *We Survived the Black Prom*, by Norma Watson (Published in the August, 1980, issue of *The Reader's Digest* as a 'Drama in Real Life' article):

. . . and it happened so quickly that no one really knew what was happening. We were all standing and applauding and singing the school song. Then—I was at the usher's table just inside the main doors, looking at the stage—there was a sparkle as the big lights over the stage apron reflected on something metallic. I was standing with Tina Blake and Stella Horan, and I think they saw it, too.

All at once there was a huge red splash in the air. Some of it hit the mural and ran in long drips. I knew right away, even before it hit them, that it was blood. Stella Horan thought it was paint, but I had a premonition, just like the time my brother got hit by a hay truck.

They were drenched. Carrie got it the worst. She looked exactly like she had been dipped in a bucket of red paint. She just sat there. She never moved. The band that was closest to the stage, Josie and the moonglows, got splattered. The lead guitarist had a white instrument, and it splattered all over it.

I say: 'My God, that's blood!'

When I said that, Tina screamed. It was very loud, and it rang out clearly in the auditorium.

People had stopped singing and everything was completely quiet. I couldn't move. I was rooted to the spot. I looked up and there were two buckets dangling high over the thrones, swinging and banging together. They were still dripping. All of a sudden they fell, with a lot of loose string paying out behind them. One of them hit Tommy Ross on the head. It made a very loud noise, like a gong.

That made someone laugh. I don't know who it was, but it wasn't the way a person laughs when they see something funny and gay. It was raw and hysterical and awful.

At the same instant, Carrie opened her eyes wide.

That was when they all started laughing. I did too. God help me. It was so . . . weird.

When I was a little girl I had a Walt Disney storybook called *Song of the South,* and it had that Uncle Remus story about the tarbaby in it. There was a picture of the tarbaby sitting in the middle of the road, looking like one of those old-time Negro minstrels with the blackface and great white eyes. When Carrie opened her eyes it was like that. They were the only part of her that wasn't completely red. And the light had gotten in them and

154

made them glassy. God help me, but she looked for all the world like Eddie Cantor doing that pop-eyed act of his.

That was what made people laugh. We couldn't help it. It was one of those things where you laugh or go crazy. Carrie had been the butt of every joke for so long, and we all felt that we were part of somethong special that night. It was as if we were watching a person rejoin the human race, and I for one thanked the Lord for it. And *that* happened. That horror.

And so there was nothing else to do. It was either laugh or cry, and who could bring himself to cry over Carrie after all those years?

She just sat there, staring out at them, and the laughter kept swelling, getting louder and louder. People were holding their bellies and doubling up and pointing at her. Tommy was the only one who wasn't looking at her. He was sort of slumped over in his seat as if he'd gone to sleep. You couldn't tell he was hurt, though: he was splashed too bad.

And then her face . . . broke. I don't know how else to describe it. She put her hands up to her face and half-staggered to her feet. She almost got tangled in her own feet and fell over, and that made people laugh even more. Then she sort of . . . hopped off the stage. It was like watching a big red frog hopping off a lily pad. She almost fell again, but kept on her feet.

Miss Desjardin came running over to her, and she wasn't laughing any more. She was holding out her arms to her. But then she veered off and hit the wall beside the stage. It was the strangest thing. She didn't stumble or anything. It was as if someone had pushed her, but there was no one there.

Carrie ran through the crowd with her hands clutching her face, and somebody put his foot out. I don't know who it was, but she went sprawling on her face, leaving a long red streak on the floor. And she said, 'Ooof!' I remember that. It made me laugh even harder, hearing Carrie say Oof like that. She started to crawl along the floor and then she got up and ran out. She ran right past me. You could smell the blood. It smelled like something sick and rotted.

She went down the stairs two at a time and then out the doors. And was gone.

The laughter just sort of faded off, a little at a time. Some people were still hitching and snorting. Lennie Brock had taken out a big white handkerchief and was wiping his eyes. Sally McManus looked all white, like she was going to throw up, but she was still giggling and she couldn't seem to stop. Billy Bosnan was just standing there with his little conductor's stick in his hand and shaking his head. Mr Lublin was sitting by Miss Desjardin and calling for a Kleenex. She had a bloody nose.

You have to understand that all this happened in no more than two minutes. Nobody could put it all together. We were stunned. Some of them were wandering around, talking a little, but not much. Helen Shyres burst into tears, and that made some of the others start up.

Then someone yelled: 'Call a doctor! Hey, call a doctor quick!'

It was Josie Vreck. He was up on the stage, kneeling by Tommy Ross, and his face was white as paper. He tried to pick him up, and the throne fell over and Tommy rolled on to the floor.

Nobody moved. They were all just staring. I felt like I was frozen in ice. My God, was all I could think. My God, my God, my God. And then this other thought crept in, and it was as if it wasn't my own at all. I was thinking about Carrie. And about God. It was all twisted up together, and it was awful.

Stella looked over at me and said: 'Carrie's back.'

And I said: 'Yes, that's right.'

The lobby doors all slammed shut. The sound was like hands clapping. Somebody in the back screamed, and that started the stampede. They ran for the doors in a rush. I just stood there, not believing it. And when I looked, just before the first of them got there and started to push, I saw Carrie looking in, her face all smeared, like an Indian with war paint on.

She was smiling.

They were pushing at the doors, hammering on them, but they wouldn't budge. As more of them crowded up against them, I could see the first ones to get there being battered against them, grunting and wheezing. They wouldn't open, and those doors are never locked. It's a state law.

Mr Stephens and Mr Lublin waded in, and began to pull them away, grabbing jackets, shorts, anything. They were all screaming and burrowing like cattle. Mr Stephens slapped a couple of girls and punched Vic Mooney in the eye. They were yelling for them to go out the back fire doors. Some did. Those were the ones who lived.

That's when it started to rain . . . at least, that's what I thought it was at first. There was water falling all over the place. I looked up and all the sprinklers were on, all over the gym. Water was hitting the basketball court and splashing. Josie Vreck was yelling for the guys in his band to turn off the electric amps and mikes quick, but they were all gone. He jumped down from the stage.

The panic at the doors stopped. People backed away, looking up at the ceiling. I heard somebody—Don Farnham, I think—say: 'This is gonna wreck the basketball court.'

A few other people started to go over and look at

Tommy Ross. All at once I knew I wanted to get out of there. I took Tina Blake's hand and said, 'Let's run. Quick.'

To get to the fire doors, you had to go down a short corridor to the left of the stage. There were sprinklers there too, but they weren't on. And the doors were open—I could see a few people running out. But most of them were just standing around in little groups, blinking at each other. Some of them were looking at the smear of blood where Carrie fell down, the water was washing it away.

I took Tina's hand and started to pull her toward the EXIT sign. At that same instant there was a huge flash of light, a scream, and a horrible feedback whine. I looked around and saw Josie Vreck holding on to one of the mike stands. He couldn't let go. His eyes were bugging out and his hair was on end and it looked like he was dancing. His feet were sliding around in the water and smoke started to come out of his shirt.

He fell over on one of the amps—they were big ones, five or six feet high—and it fell into the water. The feedback went up to a scream that was head-splitting, and then there was another sizzling flash and it stopped. Josie's shirt was on fire.

'Run!' Tina yelled at me. 'Come on, Norma, *Please!*'

We ran out into the hallway, and something exploded backstage—the main power switches, I guess. For just a second I looked back. You could see right out on to the stage, where Tommy's body was, because the curtain was up. All the heavy light cables were in the air, flowing and jerking and writhing like snakes out of an Indian fakir's basket. Then one of them pulled in two. There was a violent flash when it hit the water, and then everybody was screaming at once.

Then we were out the door and running across the parking lot. I think I was screaming. I don't remember

158

very well. I don't remember anything very well after they started screaming. After those high-voltage cables hit that water-covered floor . . .

For Tommy Ross, age eighteen, the end came swiftly and mercifully and almost without pain.

He was never even aware that something of importance was happening. There was a clanging, clashing noise that he associated momentarily with

(there go the milk buckets)

a childhood memory of his Uncle Galen's farm and then with

(somebody dropped something)

the band below him. He caught a glimpse of Josie Vreck looking over his head

(what have i got a halo or something)

and then the quarter-full bucket of blood struck him. The raised lip along the bottom of the rim struck him on top of the head and

(hey that hurt)

he went swiftly down into unconsciousness. He was still sprawled on the stage when the fire originating in the electrical equipment of Josie and the Moonglows spread to the mural of the Venetian boatman, and then to the rat warren of old uniforms, books, and papers backstage and overhead.

He was dead when the oil tank exploded a half hour later.

From the New England AP ticker, 10:46 P.M.:

CHAMBERLAIN, MAINE (AP)

A FIRE IS RAGING OUT OF CONTROL AT EWEN (U-WIN) CONSOLIDATED HIGH SCHOOL AT THIS TIME. A SCHOOL DANCE WAS IN PROGRESS AT THE TIME OF THE OUTBREAK WHICH IS BELIEVED TO HAVE BEEN

ELECTRICAL IN ORIGIN. WITNESSES SAY THAT THE SCHOOL'S SPRINKLER SYSTEM WENT ON WITHOUT WARNING, CAUSING A SHORT-CIRCUIT IN THE EQUIPMENT OF A ROCK BAND. SOME WITNESSES ALSO REPORT BREAKS IN MAIN POWER CABLES. IT IS BELIEVED THAT AS MANY AS ONE HUNDRED AND TEN PERSONS MAY BE TRAPPED IN THE BLAZING SCHOOL GYMNASIUM. FIRE FIGHTING EQUIPMENT FROM THE NEIGHBOURING TOWNS OF WESTOVER, MOTTON, AND LEWISTON HAVE REPORTEDLY RECEIVED REQUESTS FOR ASSISTANCE AND ARE NOW OR SHORTLY WILL BE EN ROUTE. AS YET, NO CASUALTIES HAVE BEEN REPORTED. ENDS.
10:46 PM MAY 27 6904D AP

From the New England AP ticker, 11:22 P.M.

URGENT

CHAMBERLAIN, MAINE (AP)

A TREMENDOUS EXPLOSION HAS ROCKED THOMAS EWIN (U-WIN) CONSOLIDATED HIGH SCHOOL IN THE SMALL MAINE TOWN OF CHAMBERLAIN. THREE CHAMBERLAIN FIRE TRUCKS, DISPATCHED EARLIER TO FIGHT A BLAZE AT THE GYMNASIUM WHERE A SCHOOL PROM WAS TAKING PLACE, HAVE ARRIVED TO NO AVAIL. ALL FIRE HYDRANTS IN THE AREA HAVE BEEN VANDALIZED, AND WATER PRESSURE FROM CITY MAINS IN THE AREA FROM SPRING STREET TO GRASS PLAZA IS REPORTED TO BE NIL. ONE FIRE OFFICIAL SAID: 'THE DAMN THINGS WERE STRIPPED OF THEIR NOZZLES, THEY MUST HAVE SPOUTED LIKE GUSHERS WHILE THOSE KIDS WERE BURNING.' THREE BODIES HAVE BEEN RECOVERED SO FAR. ONE HAS BEEN IDENTIFIED AS THOMAS B. MEARS, A CHAMBERLAIN FIREMAN. THE TWO OTHERS WERE APPARENT PROM-GOERS. THREE MORE CHAMBERLAIN FIREMEN HAVE

BEEN TAKEN TO MOTTON RECEIVING HOSPITAL
SUFFERING FROM MINOR BURNS AND SMOKE
INHALATION. IT IS BELIEVED THAT THE EXPLOSION
OCCURRED WHEN THE FIRE REACHED THE SCHOOL'S
FUEL-OIL TANKS, WHICH ARE SITUATED NEAR THE
GYMNASIUM. THE FIRE ITSELF IS BELIEVED TO HAVE
STARTED IN POORLY INSULATED ELECTRICAL
EQUIPMENT FOLLOWING A SPRINKLER SYSTEM
MALFUNCTION. ENDS.
11:22 PM MAY 27 70119E AP

Sue had only a driver's permit, but she took the keys to
her mother's car from the pegboard beside the refriger-
ator and ran to the garage. The kitchen clock read exactly
11:00.

She flooded the car on her first try, and forced herself to
wait before trying again. This time the motor coughed
and caught, and she roared out of the garage heedlessly,
dinging one fender. She turned around, and the rear
wheels splurted gravel. Her mother's '77 Plymouth
swerved on to the road, almost fishtailing on to the
shoulder and making her feel sick to her stomach. It was
only at this point that she realized she was moaning deep
in her throat, like an animal in a trap.

She did not pause at the stop sign that marked the
intersection of Route 6 and the Back Chamberlain Road.
Fire sirens filled the night in the east, where Chamberlain
bordered Westover, and from the south behind her—
Motton.

She was almost at the base of the hill when the school
exploded.

She jammed on the power brakes with both feet and
was thrown into the steering wheel like a rag doll. The
tyres wailed on the pavement. Somehow she fumbled the
door open and was out, shading her eyes against the glare.

A gout of flame had ripped skyward, trailing a nimbus of fluttering steel roof panels, wood, and paper. The smell was thick and oily. Main Street was lit as if by a flashgun. In that terrible hallway between seconds, she saw that the entire gymnasium wing of Ewen High was a gutted, flaming ruin.

Concussion struck a moment later, knocking her backwards. Road litter blew past her on a sudden and tremendous rush, along with a blast of warm air that reminded her fleetingly of

(the smell of subways)

a trip she had taken to Boston the year before. The windows of Bill's Home Drugstore and the Kelly Fruit Company jingled and fell inward.

She had fallen on her side, and the fire lit the street with hellish noonday. What happened next happened in slow motion as her mind ran steadily onward

(dead are they all dead carrie why think carrie)

at its own clip. Cars were rushing toward the scene, and some people were running in robes, nightshorts, pyjamas. She saw a man come out of the front door of Chamberlain's combined police station and courthouse. He was moving slowly. The cars were moving slowly. Even the people running were moving slowly.

She saw the man on the police-station steps cup his hands around his mouth and scream something; unclear over the shrieking town whistle, the fire sirens, the monster-mouth of fire. Sounded like:

'Heyret! Don't hey that ass!'

The street was all wet down there. The light danced on the water. Down by Teddy's Amoco station.

'—hey, that's—'

And then the world exploded.

From the sworn testimony of Thomas K. Quillan, taken before The State Investigatory Board of Maine in connection with the events of May 27-28 in Chamberlain, Maine (abridged version which follows is from *Black Prom: The White Commission Report*, Signet Books: New York, 1980):

Q. Mr Quillan, are you a resident of Chamberlain?

A. Yes.

Q. What is your address?

A. I got a room over the pool hall. That's where I work. I mop the floors, vacuum the tables, work on the machines—pinball machines, you know.

Q. Where were you on the night of May twenty-seventh at 10.30 P.M., Mr Quillan?

A. Well . . . actually, I was in a detention cell at the police station. I get paid on Thursdays, see. And I always go out and get bombed. I go out to The Cavalier, drink some Schlitz, play a little poker out back. But I get mean when I drink. Feels like the Roller Derby's going on in my head. Bummer, huh? Once I conked a guy over the head with a chair and—

Q. Was it your habit to go to the police station when you felt these fits of temper coming on?

A. Yeah. Big Otis, he's a friend of mine.

Q. Are you referring to Sheriff Otis Doyle of this county?

A. Yeah. He told me to pop in any time I started feeling mean. The night before the prom, a bunch of us guys were in the back room down at The Cavalier playing stud poker and I got to thinking Fast Marcel Dubay was cheating. I would have known better sober—a Frenchman's idea of pullin' a fast one is to look at his own cards— but that got me going. I'd had a couple of beers, you know, so I folded my hand and went on down to the

163

station. Plessy was catching, and he locked me right up in Holding Cell number 1. Plessy's a good boy. I knew his mom, but that was many years ago.

Q. Mr Quillan, do you suppose we could discuss the night of the twenty-seventh? 10:30 P.M.?

A. Ain't we?

Q. I devoutly hope so. Continue.

A. Well, Plessy locked me up around quarter to two on Friday morning, and I popped right off to sleep. Passed out, you might say. Woke up around four o'clock the next afternoon, took three Alka-Seltzers, and went back to sleep. I got a knack that way. I can sleep until my hangover's all gone. Big Otis says I should find out how I do it and take out a patent. He says I could save the world a lot of pain.

Q. I'm sure you could, Mr Quillan. Now when did you wake up again?

A. Around ten o'clock on Friday night. I was pretty hungry, so I decided to go get some chow down at the diner.

Q. They left you all alone in an open cell?

A. Sure. I'm a fantastic guy when I'm sober. In fact, one time—

Q. Just tell the committee what happened when you left the cell.

A. The fire whistle went off, that's what happened. Scared the bejesus out of me. I ain't heard that whistle at night since the Viet Nam war ended. So I ran upstairs and sonofabitch, there's no one in the office. I say to myself, hot damn, Plessy's gonna get it for this. There's always supposed to be somebody catching, in case there's a call-in. So I went over to the window and looked out.

Q. Could the school be seen from that window?

A. Yeah. People were running around and yelling. And that's when I saw Carrie White.

164

Q. Had you ever seen Carrie White before?

A. Nope.

Q. Then how did you know it was she?

A. That's hard to explain.

Q. Could you see her clearly?

A. She was standing under a street light, by the fire hydrant on the corner of Main and Spring.

Q. Did something happen?

A. I guess to Christ. The whole top of the hydrant exploded off three different ways. Left, right, and straight up to heaven.

Q. What time did this . . . uh . . . malfunction occur?

A. Around twenty to eleven. Couldn't have been no later.

Q. What happened then?

A. She started downtown. Mister, she looked awful. She was wearing some kind of party dress, what was left of it, and she was all wet from that hydrant and covered with blood. She looked like she just crawled out of a car accident. But she was *grinning*. I never saw such a grin. It was like a death's head. And she kept looking at her hands and rubbing them on her dress, trying to get the blood off and thinking she'd never get it off and how she was going to pour blood on the whole town and make them pay. It was awful stuff.

Q. How would you have any idea what she was thinking?

A. I don't know. I can't explain.

Q. For the remainder of your testimony, I wish you would stick to what you *saw,* Mr Quillan.

A. Okay. There was a hydrant on the corner of Grass Plaza, and that one went, too. I could see that one better. The big lug nuts on the sides were unscrewing themselves. I *saw* that happening. It blew, just like the other one. And she was *happy*. She was saying to herself, *that'll* give 'em a shower, *that'll* . . . whoops, sorry. The fire trucks started to go by then, and I lost track of her. The new pumper pulled up to the school and they started on those hydrants and saw they wasn't going to get no water. Chief Burton was hollering at them, and that's when the school exploded. Je-*sus*.

Q. Did you leave the police station?

A. Yeah. I wanted to find Plessy and tell him about that crazy broad and the fire hydrants. I glanced over at Teddy's Amoco, and I seen something that made my blood run cold. All six gas pumps was off their hooks. Teddy Duchamp's been dead since 1968, God love him, but his boy locked those pumps up every night just like Teddy himself used to do. Every one of them Yale padlocks was hanging busted by their hasps. The nozzles were laying on the tarmac, and the automatic feeds was set on every one. Gas was pouring out on to the sidewalk and into the street. Holy mother of God, when I seen that, my balls drew right up. Then I saw this guy running along with a lighted cigarette.

Q. What did you do?

A. Hollered at him. Something like *Hey! Watch that cigarette! Hey, don't, that's gas!* He never heard me. Fire sirens and the town whistle and cars rip-assing up and down the street, I don't wonder. I saw he was going to pitch it, so I started to duck back inside.

Q. What happened next?

A. Next? Why, next thing, the Devil came to Chamberlain . . .

When the buckets fell, she was at first only aware of a loud, metallic clang cutting through the music, and then she was deluged in warmth and wetness. She closed her eyes instinctively. There was a grunt from beside her, and in the part of her mind that had come so recently awake, she sensed brief pain.

166

(tommy)

The music came to a crashing, discordant halt, a few voices hanging on after it like broken strings, and in the sudden deadness of anticipation, filling the gap between event and realization, like doom, she heard someone say quite clearly:

'My God, that's blood.'

A moment later, as if to ram the truth of it home, to make it utterly and exactly clear, someone screamed.

Carrie sat with her eyes closed and felt the black bulge of terror rising in her mind. Momma had been right, after all. They had taken her again, gulled her again, made her the butt again. The horror of it should have been monotonous, but it was not; they had gotten her up here, up here in front of the whole school, and had repeated the shower-room scene . . . only the voice had said

(my god that's blood)

something too awful to be contemplated. If she opened her eyes and it was true, oh, what then? What then?

Someone began to laugh, a solitary, affrighted hyena sound, and she *did* open her eyes, opened them to see who it was and it *was* true, the final nightmare, she was red and dripping with it, they had drenched her in the very secretness of blood, in front of all of them and her thought

(oh . . . i . . . *COVERED* . . . with it)

was coloured a ghastly purple with her revulsion and her shame. She could smell herself and it was the *stink* of blood, the awful wet, coppery smell. In a flickering kaleidoscope of images she saw the blood running thickly down her naked thighs, hear the constant beating of the shower on the tiles, felt the soft patter of tampons and napkins against her skin as voices exhorted her to plug it UP, tasted the plump, fulsome bitterness of horror. They had finally given her the shower they wanted.

A second voice joined the first, and was followed by a

third—girl's soprano giggle—a fourth, a fifth, six, a dozen, all of them, all laughing. Vic Mooney was laughing. She could see him. His face was utterly frozen, shocked, but that laughter issued forth just the same.

She sat quite still, letting the noise wash over her like surf. They were still all beautiful and there was still enchantment and wonder, but she had crossed a line and now the fairy tale was green with corruption and evil. In this one she would bite a poison apple, be attacked by trolls, be eaten by tigers.

They were laughing at her again.

And suddenly it broke. The horrible realization of how badly she had been cheated came over her, and a horrible, soundless cry

(they're LOOKING at me)

tried to come out of her. She put her hands over her face to hide it and staggered out of the chair. Her only thought was to run, to get out of the light, to let the darkness have her and hide her.

But it was like trying to run through molasses. Her traitor mind had slowed time to a crawl; it was as if God had switched the whole scene from 78 rpm to 33⅓. Even the laughter seemed to have deepened and slowed to a sinister bass rumble.

Her feet tangled in each other, and she almost fell off the edge of the stage. She recovered herself, bent down, and hopped down to the floor. The grinding laughter swelled louder. It was like rocks rubbing together.

She wanted not to see, but she *did* see; the lights were too bright and she could see all their faces. Their mouths, their teeth, their eyes. She could see her own gore-streaked hands in front of her face.

Miss Desjardin was running toward her, and Miss Desjardin's face was filled with lying compassion. Carrie could see beneath the surface to where the *real* Miss Geer was giggling and chuckling with rancid old-maid ribaldry. Miss Desjardin's mouth opened and her voice issued forth, horrible and slow and deep:

'Let me help you, dear. Oh I am so sor—'

She struck out at her

(*flex*)

and Miss Desjardin went flying to rattle off the wall at the side of the stage and fall into a heap.

Carrie ran. She ran through the middle of them. Her hands were to her face but she could see through the prison of her fingers, could see them, how they were, beautiful, wrapped in light, swathed in the bright, angelic robes of Acceptance. The shined shoes, the clear faces, the careful beauty-parlour hairdos, the glittery gowns. They stepped back from her as if she was plague, but they kept laughing, then a foot was stuck slyly out

(o yes that comes next o yes)

and she fell over on her hands and knees and began to crawl, to crawl along the floor with her blood-clotted hair hanging in her face, crawling like St Paul on the Damascus Road, whose eyes had been blinded by the light. Next someone would kick her ass.

But no one did and then she was scrabbling to her feet again. Things began to speed up. She was out through the door, out into the lobby, then flying down the stairs that she and Tommy had swept up so grandly two hours ago.

(tommy's dead full price paid full price for bringing a plague into the place of light)

She went down them in great, awkward leaps, with the sound of the laughter flapping around her like black birds.

Then, darkness.

She fled across the school's wide front lawn, losing both of her prom slippers and fleeing barefoot. The closely cut school lawn was like velvet, lightly dusted with dewfall, and the laughter was behind her. She began to calm slightly.

Then her feet *did* tangle and she fell at full length out by the flagpole. She lay quiescent, breathing raggedly, her hot face buried in the cool grass. The tears of shame began to flow, as hot and as heavy as that first flow of menstrual blood had been. They had beaten her, bested her, once and for all time. It was over.

She would pick herself up very soon now, and sneak home by the back streets, keeping to the shadows in case someone came looking for her, find Momma, admit she had been wrong—

(!! NO !!)

The steel in her— and there was a great deal of it— suddenly rose up and cried the word out strongly. The closet? The endless, wandering prayers? The tracts and the cross and only the mechanical bird in the Black Forest cuckoo clock to mark off the rest of the hours and days and years and decades of her life?

Suddenly, as if a videotape machine had been turned on in her mind, she saw Miss Desjardin running toward her, and saw her thrown out of her way like a rag doll as she used her mind on her, without even consciously thinking of it.

She rolled over on her back, eyes staring wildly at the stars from her painted face. She was forgetting

(!! THE POWER !!)

It was time to teach them a lesson. Time to show them a thing or two. She giggled hysterically. It was one of Momma's pet phrases.

(momma coming home putting her purse down eyeglasses flashing well i guess i showed that elt a thing or two at the shop today)

There was the sprinkler system. She could turn it on,

turn it on easily. She giggled again and got up, began to walk barefoot back toward the lobby doors. Turn on the sprinkler system and close all the doors. Look in and let them *see* her looking in, watching and laughing while the shower ruined their dresses and their hairdos and took the shine off their shoes. Her only regret was that it couldn't be blood.

The lobby was empty. She paused halfway up the stairs and *FLEX*, the doors all slammed shut under the concentrated force she directed at them the pneumatic door-closers snapping off. She heard some of them scream and it was music, sweet soul music.

For a moment nothing changed and then she could feel them pushing against the doors, wanting them to open. The pressure was negligible. They were trapped

(trapped)

and the word echoed intoxicatingly in her mind. They were under her thumb, in her power. *Power!* What a word that was!

She went the rest of the way up and looked in and George Dawson was smashed up against the glass, struggling, pushing, his face distorted with effort. There were others behind him, and they all looked like fish in an aquarium.

She glanced up and yes, there were the sprinkler pipes, with their tiny nozzles like metal daisies. The pipes went through small holes in the green cinderblock wall. There were a great many inside, she remembered. Fire laws, or something.

Fire laws. In a flash her mind recalled

(black thick cords like snakes)

the power cords strung all over the stage. They were out of the audience's sight, hidden by the footlights, but she had had to step carefully over them to get to the throne. Tommy had been holding her arm.

(fire and water)

She reached up with her mind, felt the pipes, traced them. Cold; full of water. She tasted iron in her mouth, cold wet metal, the taste of water drunk from the nozzle of a garden hose.

Flex

For a moment nothing happened. Then they began to back away from the doors, looking around. She walked to the small oblong of glass in the middle door and looked inside.

It was raining in the gym.

Carrie began to smile.

She hadn't gotten all of them, only some. But she found that by looking up at the sprinkler system with her eyes, she could trace its course more easily with her mind. She began to turn on more of the nozzles, and more. Yet it wasn't enough. They weren't crying yet, so it wasn't enough

(hurt them then hurt them)

There was a boy up on the stage by Tommy, gesturing wildly and shouting something. As she watched, he climbed down and ran toward the rock band's equipment. He caught hold one of the microphone stands and was transfixed. Carrie watched, amazed, as his body went through a nearly motionless dance of electricity. His feet shuffled in the water, his hair stood up in spikes, and his mouth jerked open, like the mouth of a fish. He looked funny. She began to laugh.

(by christ then let them all look funny)

And in a sudden, blind thrust, she yanked at all the power she could feel.

Some of the lights puffed out. There was a dazzling flash somewhere as a live power cord hit a puddle of water. There were dull thumps in her mind as circuit breakers went into hopeless operation. The boy who had

172

been holding the mike stand fell over on one of his amps and there was an explosion of purple sparks and then the crepe bunting that faced the stage was burning.

Just below the thrones, a live 220-volt electricity cable was crackling on the floor and beside it Rhonda Simard was doing a crazed puppet dance in her green tulle formal. Its full skirt suddenly blazed into flame and she fell forward, still jerking.

It might have been at that moment that Carrie went over the edge. She leaned against the doors, her heart pumping wildly, yet her body as cold as ice cubes. Her face was livid, but dull red fever spots stood on each cheek. Her head throbbed thickly, and conscious thought was lost.

She reeled away from the doors, still holding them shut, doing it without thought or plan. Inside the fire was brightening and she realized dimly that the mural must have caught on fire.

She collapsed on the top step and put her head down on her knees, trying to slow her breathing. They were trying to get out the doors again, but she held them shut easily— that alone was no strain. Some obscure sense told her that a few were getting out the fire doors, but let them. She would get them later. She would get all of them. Every last one.

She went down the stairs slowly and out the front doors, still holding the gymnasium doors closed. It was easy. All you had to do was see them in your mind.

The town whistle went off suddenly, making her scream and put her hands in front of her face

(the whistle it's just the fire whistle)

for a moment. Her mind's eye lost sight of the gymnasium doors and some of them almost got out. No, no. Naughty. She slammed them shut again, catching somebody's fingers—it felt like Dale Norbert—in the jamb and severing one of them.

173

She began to reel across the lawn again, a scarecrow figure with bulging eyes, toward Main Street. On her right was dowtown—the department store, the Kelly Fruit, the beauty parlour and barbershop, gas stations, police station, fire station—

(they'll put out my fire)

But they wouldn't. She began to giggle and it was an insane sound: triumphant, lost, victorious, terrified. She came to the first hydrant and tried to twist the huge painted lug nut on the side.

(ohuh)

It was heavy. It was very heavy. Metal twisted tight to balk here. Didn't matter.

She twisted harder and felt it give. Then the other side. Then the top. Then she twisted all three at once, standing back, and they unscrewed in a flash. Water exploded outward and upward, one of the lug nuts flying five feet in front of her at suicidal speed. It hit the street, caromed high into the air, and was gone. Water gushed with white pressure in a cruciform pattern.

Smiling, staggering, her heart beating at over two hundred per minute, she began to to walk down toward Grass Plaza. She was unaware that she was scrubbing her bloodied hands against her dress like Lady Macbeth, or that she was weeping even as she laughed, or that one hidden part of her mind was keening over her final and utter ruin.

Because she was going to take them with her, and there was going to be a great burning, until the land was full of its stink.

She opened the hydrant at Grass Plaza, and then began to walk down to Teddy's Amoco. It happened to be the first gas station she came to, but it was not the last.

From the sworn testimony of Sheriff Otis Doyle, taken

before The State Investigatory Board of Maine (from *The White Commission Report*), pp. 29-31:

Q. Sheriff, where were you on the night of May twenty-seventh?

A. I was on Route 179, known as Old Bentown Road, investigating an automobile accident. This was actually over the Chamberlain town line and into Durham, but I was assisting Mel Crager, who is the Durham constable.

Q. When were you first informed that trouble had broken out at Ewen High School?

A. I received a radio transmission from Officer Jacob Plessy at 10:21.

Q. What was the nature of the radio call?

A. Officer Plessy said there was trouble at the school, but he didn't know if it was serious or not. There was a lot of shouting going on, he said, and someone had pulled a couple of fire alarms. he said He was going over to try and determine the nature of the trouble.

Q. Did he say the school was on fire?

A. No, sir.

Q. Did you ask him to report back to you?

A. I did.

Q. Did Officer Plessy report back?

A. No. He was killed in the subsequent explosion of Teddy's Amoco gas station on the corner of Main and Summer.

Q. When did you next have a radio communication concerning Chamberlain?

A. At 10:42. I was at that time returning to Chamberlain with a suspect in the back of my car—a drunk driver. As I have said, the case was actually in Mel Crager's town, but Durham has no jail. When I got him to Chamberlain, we didn't have much of one, either.

Q. What communication did you receive at 10:42?

A. I got a call from the State police that had been relayed from the Motton Fire Department. The State Police dispatcher said there was a fire and an apparent riot at Ewen High School, and a probable explosion. No one was sure of anything at that time. Remember, it all happened in a space of forty minutes.

Q. We understand that Sheriff. What happened then?

A. I drove back to Chamberlain with siren and flasher. I was trying to raise Jake Plessy and not having any luck. That's when Tom Quillan came on and started to babble about the whole town going up in flames and no water.

Q. Do you know what time that was?

A. Yes, sir. I was keeping a record by then. It was 10:58.

Q. Quillan claims the Amoco station exploded at 11:00.

A. I'd take the average, sir. Call it 10:59.

Q. At what time did you arrive in Chamberlain?

A. At 11:10 P.M.

Q. What was your immediate impression upon arriving, Sheriff Doyle?

A. I was stunned. I couldn't believe what I was seeing.

Q. What exactly *were* you seeing?

A. The entire upper half of the town's business section was burning. The Amoco station was gone. Woolworth's was nothing but a blazing frame. The fire had spread to three wooden store fronts next to that—Duffy's Bar and Grille, The Kelly Fruit Company, and the billiard parlour. The heat was ferocious. Sparks were flying on to the roofs of The Maitland Real Estate Agency and Doug Brann's Western Auto Store. Fire trucks were coming in, but they could do very little. Every fire hydrant on that side of the street was stripped. The only trucks doing any business at all were two old volunteer fire department pumpers from Westover, and about all they could do was

176

wet the roofs of the surrounding buildings. And of course the high school. It was just . . . gone. Of course it's fairly isolated—nothing close enough to it to burn—but my God, all those kids inside . . . all those kids . . .

Q. Did you meet Susan Snell upon entering town?

A. Yes, sir. She flagged me down.

Q. What time was this?

A. Just as I entered . . . 11:12, no later.

Q. What did she say?

A. She was distraught. She'd been in a minor car accident—skidding—and she was barely making sense. She asked me if Tommy was dead. I asked her who Tommy was, but she didn't answer. She asked me if we had caught Carrie yet.

Q. The Commission is extremely interested in this part of your testimony, Sheriff Doyle.

A. Yes, sir, I know that.

Q. How did you respond to her question?

A. Well, there's only one Carrie in town as far as I know, and that's Margaret White's daughter. I asked her if Carrie had something to do with the fires. Miss Snell told me Carrie had done it. Those were her words. 'Carrie did it. Carrie did it.' She said it twice.

Q. Did she say anything else?

A. Yes, sir. She said: 'They've hurt Carrie for the last time.'

Q. Sheriff, are you sure she didn't say: '*We've* hurt Carrie for the last time'?

A. I am quite sure.

Q. Are you positive? One hundred per cent?

A. Sir, the town was burning around our heads. I—

Q. Had she been drinking?

A. I beg pardon?

Q. Had she been drinking? You said she had been involved in a car smash.

177

A. I believe I said a minor skidding accident.

Q. And you can't be sure she didn't say *we* instead of *they*?

A. I guess she might have, but—

Q. What did Miss Snell do then?

A. She burst into tears. I slapped her.

Q. Why did you do that?

A. She seemed hysterical.

Q. Did she quiet eventually?

A. Yes, sir. She quieted down and got control of herself pretty well, in light of the fact that her boy friend was probably dead.

Q. Did you interrogate her?

A. Well, not the way you'd interrogate a criminal, if that's what you mean. I asked her if she knew anything about what had happened. She repeated what she had already said, but in a calmer way. I asked her where she had been when the trouble began, and she told me that she had been at home.

Q. Did you interrogate her further?

A. No, sir.

Q. Did she say anything else to you?

A. Yes, sir. She asked me—begged me—to find Carrie White.

Q. What was your reaction to that?

A. I told her to go home.

Q. Thank you, Sheriff Doyle.

Vic Mooney lurched out of the shadows near the Bankers Trust drive-in office with a grin on his face. It was a huge and awful grin, a Cheshire cat grin, floating dreamily in the fireshot darkness like a trace memory of lunacy. His hair, carefully slicked down for this emcee duties, was now sticking up in a crow's nest. Tiny drops of blood were branded across his forehead from some unremembered

178

fall in his mad flight from the Spring Ball. One eye was swelled purple and screwed shut. He walked into Sheriff Doyle's squad car, bounced back like a pool ball, and grinned in at the drunk driver dozing in the back, then he turned to Doyle, who had just finished with Sue Snell. The fire cast wavering shadows of light across everything, turning the world into the maroon tones of dried blood.

As Doyle turned, Vic Mooney clutched him. He clutched Doyle as an amorous swain might clutch his lady in a hug dance. He clutched Doyle with both arms and squeezed him, all the while goggling upward into Doyle's face with his great crazed grin.

'Vic—' Doyle began.

'She pulled all the plugs,' Vic said lightly, grinning. 'Pulled all the plugs and turned on the water and buzz, buzz, buzz.'

'Vic—'

'We can't let 'em. Oh no. NoNoNo. We can't. Carrie pulled all the plugs. Rhonda Simard burnt up. *Oh Jeeeeeeeeeeesuuuuuuuuusss*—'

Doyle slapped him twice, calloused palm cracking flatly on the boy's face. The scream died with shocking suddenness, but the grin remained, like an echo of evil. It was loose and terrible.

'What happened?' Doyle said roughly. 'What happened at the school?'

'Carrie,' Vic Muttered. 'Carrie happened at the school. She . . .' He trailed off and grinned at the ground.

Doyle gave him three brisk shakes. Vic's teeth clicked together like castanets.

'What about Carrie?'

'Queen of the Prom,' Vic muttered. 'They dumped blood on her and Tommy.'

'What—'

It was 11:15. Tony's Citgo on Summer Street suddenly exploded with a great, coughing roar. The street went daylight that made them both stagger back against the police car and shield their eyes. A huge, oily cloud of fire climbed over the elms in Courthouse Park, lighting the duck pond and the Little League diamond in scarlet. Amid the hungry crackling roar that followed Doyle could hear glass and wood and hunks of gas-station cinderblock rattling back to earth. A secondary explosion followed, making them wince again. He still couldn't get it straight

(my town this is happening in my town)

that this was happening in Chamberlain, in *Chamberlain*, for God's sake, where he drank iced tea on his mother's sun porch and refereed PAL basketball and made one last cruise out Route 6 past The Cavalier before turning in at 2:30 every morning. His town was burning up.

Tom Quillan came out of the police station and ran down the sidewalk to Doyle's cruiser. His hair was standing up every which way, he was dressed in dirty green work fatigues and an undershirt and he had his loafers on the wrong feet, but Doyle thought he had never been so glad to see anyone in his life. Tom Quillan was as much Chamberlain as anything, and he was there—intact.

'Holy God,' he panted. 'Did you see *that?*'

'What's been happening?' Doyle asked curtly.

'I been monitorin' the radio,' Quillan said, 'Motton and Westover wanted to know if they should send ambulances and I said hell yes, send everything. Hearses too. Did I do right?'

'Yes.' Doyle ran his hands through his hair. 'Have you seen Harry Block?' Block was the town's Commissioner of Public Utilities, and that included water.

180

'Nope. But Chief Deighan says they got water in the old Rennet Block across town. They're laying hose now. I collared some kids, and they're settin' up a hospital in the police station. They're good boys, but they're gonna get blood on your floor, Otis.'

Otis Doyle felt unreality surge over him. Surely this conversation couldn't be happening in Chamberlain. *Couldn't.*

'That's all right, Tommy. You did right. You go back there and start calling every doctor in the phone book. I'm going over to Summer Street.'

'Okay, Otis. If you see that crazy broad, be careful.'

'Who?' Doyle was not a barking man, but now he did. Tom Quillan flinched back. 'Carrie, Carrie White.'

'Who? How do you know?'

Quillan blinked slowly. 'I dunno. It just sort of . . . came to me.'

From the national AP ticker, 11:46 P.M.:

CHAMBERLAIN, MAINE (AP)

A DISASTER OF MAJOR PROPORTIONS HAS STRUCK THE TOWN OF CHAMBERLAIN, MAINE TONIGHT. A FIRE, BELIEVED TO HAVE BEGUN AT EWEN (U-WIN) HIGH SCHOOL DURING A SCHOOL DANCE, HAS SPREAD TO THE DOWNTOWN AREA, RESULTING IN MULTIPLE EXPLOSIONS THAT HAVE LEVELLED MUCH OF THE DOWNTOWN AREA. A RESIDENTIAL AREA TO THE WEST OF THE DOWNTOWN AREA IS ALSO REPORTED TO BE BURNING. HOWEVER, MOST CONCERN AT THIS TIME IS OVER THE HIGH SCHOOL WHERE A JUNIOR-SENIOR PROM WAS BEING HELD. IT IS BELIEVED THAT MANY OF THE PROM-GOERS WERE TRAPPED INSIDE. AN ANDOVER FIRE OFFICIAL SUMMONED TO THE SCENE SAID THE KNOWN TOTAL OF DEAD STOOD AT SIXTY-SEVEN. MOST OF THEM HIGH SCHOOL STUDENTS. ASKED HOW HIGH THE TOTAL

MIGHT GO HE SAID: 'WE DON'T KNOW. WE'RE AFRAID TO GUESS. THIS IS GOING TO BE WORSE THAN THE COCONUT GROVE.' AT LAST REPORT THREE FIRES WERE RAGING OUT OF CONTROL IN THE TOWN. REPORTS OF POSSIBLE ARSON ARE UNCONFIRMED. ENDS.
11:56 PM MAY 27 8943F AP

There were no more AP reports from Chamberlain. At 12:06 A.M., a Jackson Avenue gas main was opened. At 12:17, an ambulance attendant from Motton tossed out a cigarette butt as the rescue vehicle sped toward Summer Street.

The explosion destroyed nearly half a block at a stroke, including the offices of *The Chamberlain Clarion*. By 12:18 A.M., Chamberlain was cut off from the country that slept in reason beyond.

At 12:10, still seven minutes before the gas-main explosion, the telephone exchange experienced a softer explosion: a complete jam of every town phone line still in operation. The three harried girls on duty stayed at their posts but were utterly unable to cope. They worked with expressions of wooden horror on their faces, trying to place unplaceable calls.

And so Chamberlain drifted into the streets.

They came like an invasion from the graveyard that lay in the elbow creek formed by the intersection of The Bellsqueeze Road and Route 6; they came in white nightgowns and in robes, as if in winding shrouds. They came in pyjamas and curlers (Mrs Dawson, she of the now-deceased son who had been a very funny fellow, came in a mudpack as if dressed for a minstrel show); they came to see what happened to their town, to see if it was indeed lying burnt and bleeding. Many of them also came to die.

182

Carlin Street was thronged with them, a riptide of them, moving downtown through the hectic light in the sky, when Carrie came out of the Carlin Street Congregational Church, where she had been praying.

She had gone in only five minutes before, after opening the gas main (it had been easy; as soon as she pictured it lying there under the street it had been easy), but it seemed like hours. She had prayed long and deeply, sometimes aloud, sometimes silently. Her heart thudded and laboured. The veins on her face and neck bulged. Her mind was filled with the huge knowledge of POWERS, and of an ABYSS. She prayed in front of the altar, kneeling in her wet and torn and bloody gown, her feet bare and dirty and bleeding from a broken bottle she had stepped on. Her breath sobbed in and out of her throat, and the church was filled with groanings and swayings and sunderings as psychic energy sprang from her. Pews fell, hymnals flew, and a silver Communion set cruised silently across the vaulted darkness of the nave to crash into the far wall. She prayed and there was no answering. No one was there—or if there was, He/It was cowering from her. God had turned His face away, and why not? This horror was as much His doing as hers. And so she left the church, left it to go home and find her momma and make destruction complete.

She paused on the lower step, looking at the flocks of people streaming toward the centre of town. Animals. Let them burn, then. Let the streets be filled with the smell of their sacrifice. Let this place be called racca, ichabod, wormwood.

Flex

And power transformers atop lightpoles bloomed into nacreous purple light, spitting catherine-wheel sparks. High-tension wires fell into the streets in pick-up-sticks tangles and some of them ran, and that was bad for them because now the whole street was littered with wires and the stink began, the burning began. People began to scream and back away and touched the cables and went into jerky electrical dances. Some had already slumped into the street, their robes and pyjamas smouldering.

Carrie turned back and looked fixedly at the church she had just left. The heavy door suddenly swung shut, as if in a hurricane wind.

Carrie turned towards home.

From the sworn testimony of Mrs Cora Simard, taken before The State Investigatory Board (from *The White Commission Report*). pp. 217-218:

Q. Mrs Simrad, the Board understands that you lost your daughter on Prom Night, and we sumpathize with you deeply. We will make this as brief as possible.

A. Thank you. I want to help if I can, of course.

Q. Were you on Carlin Street at approximately 12:12 when Carietta White came out of the First Congregational Church on that street?

A. Yes.

Q. Why were you there?

A. My husband had to be in Boston over the weekend on business and Rhonda was at the Spring Ball. I was home alone watching TV and waiting up for her. I was watching the Friday Night Movie when the town hall whistle went off, but I didn't connect that with the dance. But then the explosion . . . I didn't know what to do. I tried to call the police but got a busy signal after the first three numbers. I . . . I . . . Then . . .

Q. Take your time, Mrs Simard. All the time you need.

A. I was getting frantic. There was a second explosion—Teddy's Amoco station, I know now—and I

184

decided to go downtown and see what was happening. There was a glow in the sky, an awful glow. That was when Mrs Shyres pounded on the door.

Q. Mrs Georgette Shyres?

A. Yes, they live around the corner. 217 Willow. That's just off Carlin Street. She was pounding and calling: 'Cora, are you in there? Are you in there?' I went to the door. She was in her bath-robe and slippers. Her feet looked cold. She said they had called Auburn to see if they knew anything and they told her the school was on fire. I said: 'Oh dear God, Rhonda's at the dance.'

Q. Is this when you decided to go downtown with Mrs Shyres?

A. We didn't decide anything. We just went. I put on a pair of slippers—Rhonda's, I think. They had little white puffballs on them. I should have worn my shoes, but I wasn't thinking. I guess I'm not thinking now. What do you want to hear about my shoes for?

Q. You tell it in your own way, Mrs Simard.

A. T-Thank you. I gave Mrs Shyres some old jacket that was around, and we went.

Q. Were there many people walking down Carlin Street?

A. I don't know. I was too upset. Maybe thirty. Maybe more.

Q. What happened?

A. Georgette and I were walking toward Main Street, holding hands just like two little girls walking across a meadow after dark. Georgette's teeth were clicking. I remember that. I wanted to ask her to stop clicking her teeth, but I thought it would be impolite. A block and a half from the Congo Church, I saw the door open and I thought: Someone has gone in to ask God's help. But a second later I knew that wasn't true.

Q. How did you know? It would be logical to assume

185

just what you first assumed, wouldn't it?

A. I just knew.

Q. Did you know the person who came out of the church?

A. Yes. It was Carrie White.

Q. Had you ever seen Carrie White before?

A. No. She was not one of my daughter's friends.

Q. Had you ever seen a picture of Carrie White?

A. No.

Q. And in any case, it was dark and you were a block and a half from the church.

A. Yes, sir.

Q. Mrs Simard, how did you know it was Carrie White?

A. I just knew.

Q. This *knowing*, Mrs Simard: was it like a light going on in your head?

A. No, sir.

Q. What *was* it like?

A. I can't tell you. It faded away the way a dream does. An hour after you get up you can only remember you had a dream. But I knew.

Q. Was there an emotional feeling that went with this knowledge?

A. Yes. Horror.

Q. What did you do then?

A. I turned to Georgette and said: 'There she is.' Georgette said: 'Yes, that's her.' She started to say something else, and then the whole street was lit up by a bright glow and there were crackling noises and then the power lines started to fall into the street, some of them spitting live sparks. One of them hit a man in front of us and he b-burst into flames. Another man started to run and he stepped on one of them and his body just . . . arched backward, as if his back had turned into elastic.

And then *he* fell down. Other people were screaming and running, just running blindly, and more and more cables fell. They were strung all over the place like snakes. And she was glad about it. *Glad!* I could *feel* her being glad. I knew I had to keep my head. The people who were running were getting electrocuted. Georgette said: 'Quick, Cora. Oh God, I don't want to get burned alive.' I said, 'Stop that. We have to use our heads, Georgette, or we'll never use them again.' Something foolish like that. But she wouldn't listen. She let go of my hand and started to run for the sidewalk. I screamed at her to stop—there was one of those heavy main cables broken off right in front of us—but she didn't listen. And she . . . she . . . oh, I could smell her when she started to burn. Smoke just seemed to *burst* out of her clothes and I thought: that's what it must be like when someone gets electrocuted. The smell was sweet like pork. Have any of you ever smelled that? Sometimes I smell it in my dreams. I stood still, watching Georgette Shyres turn black. There was a big explosion over in the West End—the gas main, I suppose—but I never even noticed it. I looked around and I was all alone. Everyone else had either run away or was burning. I saw maybe six bodies. They were like piles of old rags. One of the cables had fallen on to the porch of a house to the left, and it was catching on fire. I could hear the old-fashioned shake shingles popping like corn. It seemed like I stood there a long time, telling myself to keep my head. It seemed like hours. I began to be afraid that I would faint and fall on one of the cables, or that I would panic and start to run. Like . . . like Georgette. So then I started to walk. One step at a time. The street got even brighter, because of the burning house. I stepped over two live wires and went around a body that wasn't much more than a puddle. I—I—I had to look to see where I was going. There was a wedding ring on the body's hand, but it was all black. All *black*. Jesus, I was thinking. Oh dear Lord. I stepped over another one and then there were three, all at once. I just stood there looking at them. I thought if I got over those I'd be all right but . . . I didn't dare. Do you know what I kept thinking of? That game you play when you're kids, Giant Step. A voice in my mind was saying, Cora, take one giant step over the live wires in the street. And I was thinking *May I? May I?* One of them was still spitting a few sparks, but the other two looked dead. But you can't tell. The third rail looks dead too. So I stood there, waiting for someone to come and nobody did. The house was still burning and the flames had spread to the lawn and the trees and the hedge beside it. But no fire trucks came. Of course they didn't. The whole west side was burning up by that time. And I felt so *faint*. And at last I knew it was take the giant step or faint and so I took it, as big a giant step as I could, and the heel of my slipper came down not an inch from the last wire. Then I got over and went around the end of one more wire and then I started to run. And that's all I remember. When morning came I was lying on a blanket in the police station with a lot of other people. Some of them—a few—were kids in their prom get-ups and I started to ask them if they had seen Rhonda. And they said . . . they s-s-said . . .

(A short recess)

Q. You are personally sure that Carrie White did this?
A. Yes.
Q. Thank you, Mrs Simard.
A. I'd like to ask a question, if you please.
Q. Of course.
A. What happens if there are others like her? What happens to the world?

From *The Shadow Exploded* (p. 151):

By 12:45 on the morning of May 28, the situation in Chamberlain was critical. The school had burned itself out on a fairly isolated piece of ground, but the entire downtown area was ablaze. Almost all the city water in that area had been tapped, but enough was available (at low pressure) from Deighan Street water mains to save the business buildings below the intersection of Main and Oak streets.

The explosion of Tony's Citgo on upper Summer Street had resulted in a ferocious fire that was not to be controlled until nearly ten o'clock that morning. There was water on Summer Street; there simply were no firemen or fire-fighting equipment to utilize it. Equipment was then on its way from Lewiston, Auburn, Lisbon and Brunswick, but nothing arrived until one o'clock.

On Carlin Street, an electrical fire, caused by downed power lines, had begun. It was eventually to gut the entire north side of the street, including the bungalow where Margaret White gave birth to her daughter.

On the west end of town, just below what is commonly called Brickyard Hill, the worst disaster had taken place: the explosion of a gas main and a resulting fire that raged out of control through most of the next day.

And if we look at these flash points on a municipal map (see page facing), we can pick out Carrie's route—a wandering, looping path of destruction through the town, but one with an almost certain destination: home . . .

Something toppled over in the living room, and Margaret White straightened up, cocking her head to one side. The butcher knife glittered dully in the light of the flames. The electric power had gone off sometime before, and the only light in the house came from the fire up the street.

189

One of the pictures fell from the wall with a thump. A moment later the Black Forest cuckoo clock fell. The mechanical bird gave a small, strangled squawk and was still.

From the town the sirens whooped endlessly, but she could still hear the footsteps when they turned up the walk.

The door blew open. Steps in the hall.

She heard the plaster plaques in the living room (CHRIST, THE UNSEEN GUEST; WHAT WOULD JESUS DO; THE HOUR DRAWETH NIGH; IF TONIGHT BECAME JUDGMENT, WOULD YOU BE READY) explode one after the other, like plaster birds in a shooting gallery.

(o i've been there and seen the harlots shimmy on wooden stages)

She sat up on her stool like a very bright scholar who has gone to the head of the class, but her eyes were deranged.

The living-room windows blew outward.

The kitchen door slammed and Carrie walked in.

Her body seemed to have become twisted, shrunken, cronelike. The prom dress was in tatters and flaps, and the pig blood had began to clot and streak. There was a smudge of grease on her forehead and both knees were scraped and raw-looking.

'Momma,' she whispered. Her eyes were preternaturally bright, hawklike, but her mouth was trembling. If someone had been there to watch, he would have been struck by the resemblance between them.

Margaret White sat on her kitchen stool, the carving knife hidden among the folds of her dress in her lap.

'I should have killed myself when he put it in me,' she said clearly. 'After the first time, before we were married, he promised. Never again. He said we just . . . slipped. I believed him. I fell down and I lost the baby and that was

God's judgment. I felt that the sin had been expiated. By blood. But sin never dies. *Sin . . . never . . . dies.*' Her eyes glittered.

'Momma, I—'

'At first it was all right. We lived sinlessly. We slept in the same bed, belly to belly sometimes, and o, I could feel the presence of the Serpent, but we never did until.' She began to grin, and it was a hard, terrible grin. 'And that night I could see him looking at me That Way. We got down on our knees to pray for strength and he . . . touched me. In that place. That woman place. And I sent him out of the house. He was gone for hours, and I prayed for him. I could see him in my mind's eye, walking the midnight streets, wrestling with the devil as Jacob wrestled with the Angel of the Lord. And when he came back, my heart was filled with thanksgiving.'

She paused, grinning her dry, spitless grin into the shifting shadows of the room.

'Momma, I don't want to hear it!'

Plates began to explode in the cupboards like clay pigeons.

'It wasn't until he came in that I smelled the whiskey on his breath. And he took me. *Took me!* With the stink of filthy roadhouse whiskey still on him he took me . . . *and I liked it!*' She screamed out the last words at the ceiling. *'I liked it o all that dirty fucking and his hands on me ALL OVER ME!'*

'MOMMA!'

(*MOMMA!!*)

She broke off as if slapped and blinked at her daughter. 'I almost killed myself,' she said in a more normal tone of voice. 'And Ralph wept and talked about atonement and I didn't and then he was dead and then I thought God had visited me with cancer; that He was turning my female parts into something as black and rotten as my sinning

191

soul. But that would have been too easy. The Lord works in mysterious ways, His wonders to perform. I see that now. When the pains began I went and got a knife—this knife—' she held it up '—and waited for you to come so I could make my sacrifice. But I was weak and backsliding. I took this knife in hand again when you were three, and I backslid again. So now the devil has come home.'

She held the knife up, and her eyes fastened hypnotically on the glittering hook of its blade.

Carrie took a slow, blundering step forward.

'I came to kill you, Momma. And you were waiting here to kill me. Momma, I . . . it's not right, Momma. It's not . . .'

'Let's pray,' Momma said softly. Her eyes fixed on Carrie's and there was a crazed, awful compassion in them. The fire light was brighter now, dancing on the walls like dervishes. 'For the last time, let us pray.'

'Oh Momma help me!' Carrie cried out.

She fell forward on her knees, head down, hands raised in supplication.

Momma leaned forward, and the knife came down in a shining arc.

Carrie, perhaps seeing out of the tail of her eye, jerked back, and instead of penetrating her back, the knife went into her shoulder to the hilt. Momma's feet tangled in the legs of her chair, and she collapsed in a sitting sprawl.

They stared at each other in silent tableau.

Blood began to ooze from around the handle of the knife and to splash on to the floor.

Then Carrie said softly: 'I'm going to give you a present, Momma.'

Margaret tried to get up, staggered, and fell back on her hands and knees. 'What are you doing?' she croaked hoarsely.

'I'm picturing your heart, Momma,' Carrie said. 'It's

easier when you see things in your mind. Your heart is a big red muscle. Mine goes faster when I use my power. But your is going a little slower now. A little slower.'

Margaret tried to get up again, failed, and forked the sign of the evil eye at her daughter.

'A little slower, Momma. Do you know what the present is, Momma? What you always wanted. Darkness. And whatever God lives there.'

Margaret White whispered: 'Our father, Who art in heaven—'

'Slower, Momma. Slower.'

'—hallowed be Thy name—'

'I can see the blood draining back into you. Slower.'

'—Thy Kingdom come—'

'Your feet and hands like marble, like alabaster. White.'

'—Thy will be done—'

'*My* will, Momma. Slower.'

'—on earth——'

'Slower.'

'—as . . . as . . . as it . . .'

She collapsed forward, hands twitching.

'—as it is in heaven.'

Carrie whispered: 'Full stop.'

She looked down at herself, and put her hands weakly around the haft of the knife.

(no o no that hurts that's too much hurt)

She tried to get up, failed, then pulled herself up by Momma's stool. Dizziness and nausea washed over her. She could taste blood, bright and slick, on the back of her throat. Smoke, acrid and choking, was drifting in through the windows now. The flames had reached next door; even now sparks would be lighting softly on the roof that rocks had punched brutally through a thousand years before.

Carrie went out the back door, staggered across the lawn, and rested

(where's my momma)

against a tree. There was something she was supposed to do. Something about

(roadhouses parking lots)

the Angel with the Sword. The Fiery Sword.

Never mind. It would come to her.

She crossed by back yards to Willow Street and then crawled up the embankment to Route 6.

It was 1:15 A.M.

It was 11:20 P.M. when Christine Hargensen and Billy Nolan got back to The Cavalier. They went up the back stairs, down the hall, and before she could do more than turn on the lights, he was yanking at her blouse.

'For God's sake let me unbutton it—'

'To hell with that.'

He ripped it suddenly down the back. The cloth tore with a sudden hard sound. One button popped free and winked on the bare wood floor. Honky-tonkin' music came faintly up to them, and the building vibrated subtly with the clumsy-enthusiastic dancing of farmers and truckers and millworkers and waitresses and hairdressers, of the greasers and their townie girl friends from Westover and Motton.

'Hey—'

'Be quiet.'

He slapped her, rocking her head back. Her eyes took on a flat and deadly shine.

'This is the end, Billy.' She backed away from him, breasts swelling into her bra, flat stomach pumping, legs long and tapering in her jeans; but she backed toward the bed. 'It's over.'

'Sure,' he said. He lunged for her and she punched him,

a surprising hard punch that landed on his cheek.

He straightened and twitched his head a little. 'You gave me a shiner, you bitch.'

'I'll give you more.'

'You're goddam right you will.' They stared at each other, panting, glaring. Then he began to unbutton his shirt, a little grin beginning on his face.

'We got it on, Charlie. We really got it on.' He called her Charlie whenever he was pleased with her. It seemed to be, she thought with a cold blink of humour, a generic term for good cunt.

She felt a little smile come to her own face, relaxed a little, and that was when he whipped his shirt across her face and came in low, butting her in the stomach like a goat, tipping her on to the bed. The springs screamed. She pounded her fists helplessly on his back.

'Get off me! Get off me! Get off me! You fucking greaseball, *get off me!*'

He was grinning at her, and with one quick, hard yank her zipper was broken, her hips free.

'Call your daddy?' he was grunting. 'That what you gonna do? Huh? Huh? That it, ole Chuckie? Call big ole legal beagle daddy? Huh? I woulda done it to you, you know that? I woulda dumped it all over your fuckin squash. You know it? Huh? Know it? Pig blood for pigs, right? Right on your motherfucking squash. You—'

She had suddenly ceased to resist. He paused, staring down at her, and she had an odd smile on her face. 'You wanted it this way all along, didn't you? You miserable little scumbag. That's right, isn't it? You creepy little one-nut low-cock dinkless wonder.'

His grin was slow, crazed. 'It doesn't matter.'

'No,' she said. 'It doesn't.' Her smile suddenly vanished, the cords on her neck stood out as she hawked back—and spat in his face.

They descended into a red, thrashing unconsciousness.

Downstairs the music thumped and wheezed *('I'm poppin little white pills an my eyes are open wide/Six days on the road, and I'm gonna make it home tonight!')*, c/w, full throttle, very loud, very bad, five-man band wearing sequined cowboy shirts and new pegged jeans with bright rivets, occasionally wiping mixed sweat and Vitalis from their brows, lead guitar, rhythm, steel, dobro guitar, drums; no one heard the town whistle, or the first explosion, or the second; and when the gas main blew and the music stopped and someone drove into the parking lot and began to yell the news, Chris and Billy were asleep.

Chris woke suddenly and the clock on the night table said five minutes of one. Someone was pounding on the door.

'Billy!' the voice was yelling. 'Get up! Hey! Hey!'

Billy stirred, rolled over, and knocked the cheap alarm clock on to the floor. 'What the Christ?' he said thickly, and sat up. His back stung. The bitch had covered it with long scratches. He'd barely noticed it at the time, but now decided he was going to have to send her home bowlegged. Just to show her who was b—

Silence struck him. Silence. The Cavalier did not close until two; as a matter of fact, he could still see the neon twinkling and flicking through the dusty garret window. Except for the steady pounding

(something happened)

the place was a graveyard.

'Billy, you in there? Hey!'

'Who is it?' Chris whispered. Her eyes were glittering and watchful in the intermittent neon.

'Jackie Talbot,' he said absently, then raised his voice. 'What?'

'Lemme in, Billy. I got to talk to you!'

Billy got up and padded to the door, naked. He

unlocked the old-fashioned hook-and-eye and opened it.

Jackie Talbot burst in. His eyes were wild and his face was smeared with soot. He had been drinking it up with Steve and Henry when the news came at ten minutes of twelve. They had gone back to town in Henry's elderly Dodge convertible, and had seen the Jackson Avenue gas main explode from the vantage point of Brickyard Hill. When Jackie had borrowed the Dodge and started to drive back at 12:30, the town was a panicky shambles.

'Chamberlain's burning up,' he said to Billy. 'Whole fuckin town. The school's gone. The Centre's gone. West End blew up—gas. And Carlin Street's on fire. And they're saying Carrie White did it!'

'Oh God,' Chris said. She started to get out of bed and grope for her clothes. 'What did—'

'Shut up,' Billy said mildly, 'or I'll kick your ass.' He looked at Jackie again and nodded for him to go on.

'They seen her. Lots of people seen her. Billy, they say she's all covered with blood. She was at that fuckin prom tonight . . . Steve and Henry didn't get it but . . . Billy, did you . . . that pig blood . . . was it—'

'Yeah,' Billy said.

'Oh, no.' Jackie stumbled back against the doorframe. His face was a sickly yellow in the light of the one hall lightbulb. 'Oh Jesus, Billy, the whole town—'

'Carrie trashed the whole town? Carrie *White?* You're full of shit.' He said it calmly, almost serenely. Behind him, Chris was dressing rapidly.

'Go and look out the window,' Jackie said.

Billy went over and looked out. The entire eastern horizon had gone crimson, and the sky was alight with it. Even as he looked, three fire trucks screamed by. He could make out the names on them in the glow of the street light that marked The Cavalier's parking lot.

'Son of a whore,' he said. 'Those trucks are from Brunswick.'

'Brunswick?' Chris said. 'That's forty miles away. That can't be . . .'

Billy turned back to Jackie Talbot. 'All right. What happened?'

Jackie shook his head. 'Nobody knows, not yet. It started at the high school. Carrie and Tommy Ross got the King and Queen, and then somebody dumped a couple of buckets of blood on them and she ran out. Then the school caught on fire, and they say nobody got out. Then Teddy's Amoco blew up, then that Mobil station on Summer Street—'

'Citgo.' Billy corrected. 'It's a Citgo.'

'Who the fuck cares?' Jackie screamed. 'It was her, every place something happened it was *her!* And those buckets . . . none of us wore gloves . . .'

'I'll take care of it,' Billy said.

'You don't get it, Billy. Carrie is—'

'Get out.'

'Billy—'

'Get out or I'll break your arm and feed it to you.'

Jackie backed out of the door warily.

'Go home. Don't talk to nobody. I'm going to take care of everything.'

'All right,' Jackie said. 'Okay. Billy, I just thought—'

Billy slammed the door.

Chris was on him in a second. 'Billy what are we going to do that bitch Carrie oh my Lord what are we going to—'

Billy slapped her, getting his whole arm into it, and knocked her on to the floor. Chris sat sprawled in stunned silence for a moment, and then held her face and began to sob.

Billy put on his pants, his tee shirt, his boots. Then he

198

went to the chipped porcelain washstand in the corner, clicked on the light, wet his head, and began to comb his hair, bending down to see his reflection in the spotted, ancient mirror. Behind him, wavy and distorted, Chris Hargensen sat on the floor, wiping blood from her split lip.

'I'll tell you what we're going to do,' he said. 'We're going into town and watch the fires. Then we're coming home. You're going to tell your dear old daddy that we were out to The Cavalier drinking beers when it happened. I'm gonna tell my dear ole mummy the same thing. Dig.'

'Billy, your fingerprints,' she said. Her voice was muffled, but respectful.

'*Their* fingerprints,' he said. '*I* wore gloves.'

'Would they tell?' she asked. 'If the police took them in and questioned them—'

'Sure,' he said. 'They'd tell.' The loops and swirls were almost right. They glistened in the light of the dull, fly-specked globe like eddies on deep water. His face was calm, reposeful. The comb he used was a battered old Ace, clotted with grease. His father had given it to him on his eleventh birthday, and not one tooth was broken in it. Not one.

'Maybe they'll never find the buckets,' he said. 'If they do, maybe the fingerprints will all be burnt off. I don't know. But if Doyle takes any of 'em in, I'm heading for California. You do what you want.'

'Would you take me with you?' she asked. She looked at him from the floor, her lip puffed to negroid size, her eyes pleading.

He smiled. 'Maybe.' But he wouldn't. Not any more. 'Come on. We're going to town.'

They went downstairs and through the empty dance hall, where chairs were still pushed back and beers were standing flat on the tables.

As they went out through the fire door Billy said: 'This place sucks, anyway.'

They got into his car, and he started it up. When he popped on the headlights, Chris began to scream, hands in fists up to her cheeks.

Billy felt it at the same time: Something in his mind.

(carrie carrie carrie carrie)

a presence.

Carrie was standing in front of them, perhaps seventy feet away.

The high beams picked her out in ghastly horror-movie blacks and whites, dripping and clotted with blood. Now much of it was her own. The hilt of the butcher knife still protruded from her shoulder, and her gown was covered with dirt and grass stain. She had crawled much of the distance from Carlin Street, half fainting, to destroy this roadhouse—perhaps the very one where the doom of her creation had begun.

She stood swaying, her arms thrown out like the arms of a stage hypnotist, and she began to totter toward them.

It happened in the blink of a second. Chris had not had time to expend her first scream. Billy's reflexes were good and his reaction was instantaneous. He shifted into low, popped the clutch, and floored it.

The Chevrolet's tyres screamed against the asphalt, and the car sprang forward like some old and terrible maneater. The figure swelled in the windshield and as it did the presence became louder

(CARRIE CARRIE CARRIE)

and louder

(CARRIE CARRIE CARRIE)

like a radio being turned up to full volume. Time seemed to close around them in a frame and for a moment they were frozen even in motion: Billy

(CARRIE just like the dogs *CARRIE* just like the goddam dogs *CARRIE* brucie i wish i could *CARRIE* be *CARRIE* you)*

and Chris

(CARRIE jesus not to kill her *CARRIE* didn't mean to kill her *CARRIE* billy i dont *CARRIE* want to *CARRIE* see it *CA)*

and Carrie herself.

(see the wheel car wheel gas pedal i see the *WHEEL* o god my heart my heart my heart)

And Billy suddenly felt his car turn traitor, come alive, slither in his hands, The Chevvy dug around in a smoking half-circle, straight pipes racketing, and suddenly the clapboard side of The Cavalier was swelling, swelling, swelling and

(this is)

they slammed into it at forty, still accelerating, and wood sprayed up in a neon-tinted detonation. Billy was thrown forward and the steering column speared him. Chris was thrown into the dashboard.

The gas tank split open, and fuel began to puddle around the rear of the car. Part of one straight pipe fell into it, and the gas bloomed into flame.

Carrie lay on her side, eyes closed, panting thickly. Her chest was on fire.

She began to drag herself across the parking lot, going nowhere.

(momma i'm sorry it all went wrong o momma o please o please i hurt so bad momma what do i do)

And suddenly it didn't seem to matter any more, nothing would matter if she could turn over, turn over and see the stars, turn over and look once and die.

And that was how Sue found her at two o'clock.

When Sheriff Doyle left her, Sue walked down the street

and sat on the steps of the Chamberlain U-Wash-It. She stared at the burning sky without seeing it. Tommy was dead. She knew it was true and accepted it with an ease that was dreadful.

And Carrie had done it.

She had no idea how she knew it, but the conviction was as pure and right as arithmetic.   .

Time passed. It didn't matter. Macbeth hath murdered sleep and Carrie hath murdered time. Pretty good. A *bon mot* Sue smiled dolefully. Can this be the end of our heroine, Miss Sweet Little Sixteen? No worries about the country club and Kleen Korners now. Not ever. Gone. Burned out. Someone ran past, blabbering that Carlin Street was on fire. Good for Carlin Street. Tommy was gone. And Carrie had gone home to murder her mother.

(???????????)

She sat bolt upright, staring into the darkness.

(???????????)

She didn't know how she knew. It bore no relationship to anything she had ever read about telepathy. There were no pictures in her head, no great white flashes of revelation, only prosaic knowledge; the way you know summer follows spring, that cancer can kill you, that Carrie's mother was dead already, that—

(!!!!!)

Her heart rose thickly in her chest. Dead? She examined in her knowledge of the incident, trying to disregard the insistent weirdness of knowing from nothing.

Yes, Margaret White was dead, something to do with her heart. But she had stabbed Carrie. Carrie was badly hurt. She was—

There was nothing more.

She got up and ran back to her mother's car. Ten minutes later she parked on the corner of Branch and Carlin Street, which was on fire. No trucks were available to fight the blaze yet, but saw-horses had been put across both ends of the street, and greasily smoking roads pots lit a sign which said;

DANGER ! LIVE WIRES !

Sue cut through two back yards and forced her way through a budding hedge that scraped at her, white short, stiff bristles. She came out one yard from the White's house and crossed over.

The house was in flames, the roof blazing. It was impossible to even think about getting close enough to look in. But in the strong firelight she saw something better: the splashed trail of Carrie's blood. She followed it with her head down, past the larger spots where Carrie had rested, through another hedge, across a Willow Street back yard, and then through an undeveloped tangle of scrub pine and oak. Beyond that, a short, unpaved spur— little more than a footpath—wound up the rise of land to the right, angling away from Route 6.

She stopped suddenly as doubt struck her with vicious and corrosive force. Suppose she could find her? What then? Heart failure? Set on fire? Controlled and forced to walk in front of an oncoming car or fire engine? Her peculiar knowledge told her Carrie would be capable of all things.

(find a policeman)

She giggled a little at that one and sat down in the grass, which was silked with dew. She had already found a policeman. And even supposing Otis Doyle had believed her, what then? A mental picture came to her of a hundred desperate manhunters surrounding Carrie, demanding her to hand over her weapons and give up. Carrie obediently raises her hands and plucks her head from her shoulders. Hands it to Sheriff Doyle, who solemnly puts it in a wicker basket marked People's Exhibit A.

(and tommy's dead)

Well, well. She began to cry. She put her hands over her face and sobbed into them. A soft breeze snuffled through the juniper bushes on top of the hill. More fire engines screamed by on Route 6 like huge red hounds in the night.

(the town's burning down o well)

She had no idea how long she sat there, crying in a grainy half-doze. She was not even aware that she was following Carrie's progress toward The Cavalier, no more than she was aware of the process of respiration unless she thought about it. Carrie was hurt very badly, was going on brute determination alone at this point. It was three miles out to The Cavalier, even across-country, as Carrie was going. Sue

(watched? thought? doesn't matter)

as Carrie fell in a brook and dragged herself out, icy and shivering. It was really amazing that she kept going. But of course it was for Momma. Momma wanted her to be the Angel's Fiery Sword, to destroy—

(she's going to destroy that too)

She got up and began to run clumsily, not bothering to follow the trail of blood. She didn't need to follow it any more.

From *The Shadow Exploded* (pp. 164-165):

Whatever any of us may think of the Carrie White affair, it is over. It's time to turn to the future. As Dean McGuffin points out, in his excellent *Science Yearbook* article, if we refuse to do this, we will almost certainly have to pay the piper—and the price is apt to be a high one.

A thorny moral question is raised here. Progress is already being made toward complete isolation of the TK gene. It is more or less assumed in the scientific community (see, for instance, Bourke and Hannegan's 'A View Toward Isolation of the TK Gene with Specific

Recommendations for Control Parameters' in *Mocrobiology Annual,* Berkeley: 1982) that when a testing procedure is established, all school-age children will undergo the test as routinely as they now undergo the TB skin-patch. Yet TK is not a germ; it is as much a part of the afflicted person as the colour of his eyes.

If overt TK ability occurs as a part of puberty, and if this hypothetical TK test is performed on children entering the first grade, we shall certainly be forewarned. But in this case, is forewarned forearmed? If the TB test shows positive a child can be treated or isolated. If the TK test shows positive, we have no treatment except a bullet in the head. And how is it possible to isolate a person who will eventually have the power to knock down all walls?

And even if isolation could be made successful, would the American people allow a small, pretty girl-child to be ripped away from her parents at the first sign of puberty to be locked in a bank vault for the rest of her life? I doubt it. Especially when The White Commission has worked so hard to convince the public that the nightmare in Chamberlain was a complete fluke.

Indeed, we seem to have returned to Square One . . . .

From the sworn testimony of Susan Snell, taken before The State Investigatory Board of Maine (from *The White Commission Report*), pp. 306-472:

Q. Now, Miss Snell, the Board would like to go through your testimony concerning your alleged meeting with Carrie White in The Cavalier parking lot—

A. Why do you keep asking the same questions over and over? I've told you twice already.

Q. We want to make sure the record is correct in every—

A. You want to catch me in a lie, isn't that what you

really mean? You don't think I'm telling the truth, do you?

Q. You say you came upon Carrie at—

A. Will you answer me?

Q. —at 2:00 on the morning of May 28th. Is that correct?

A. I'm not going to answer any more questions until you answer the one I just asked.

Q. Miss Snell, this body is empowered to cite you for contempt if you refuse to answer on any other grounds than Constitutional ones.

A. I don't care what you're empowered to do. I've lost someone I love. Go and throw me in jail. I don't care. I—I—Oh, go to hell. All of you, go to hell. You're trying to . . . to . . . I don't know, crucify me or something. Just lay off me!

(A short recess)

Q. Miss Snell, are you willing to continue your testimony at this time?

A. Yes. But I won't be badgered. Mr Chairman.

Q. Of course not, young lady. No one wants to badger you. Now you claim to have come upon Carrie in the parking lot of this tavern at 2:00. Is that correct?

A. Yes.

Q. You knew it was 2:00?

A. I was wearing the watch you see on my wrist right now.

Q. To be sure. Isn't The Cavalier better than six miles from where you left your mother's car?

A. It is by the road. It's close to three as the crow flies.

Q. You walked this distance?

A. Yes.

Q. Now you testified earlier that you 'knew' you were getting close to Carrie. Can you explain this?

206

A. No.

Q. Could you smell her?

A. What?

Q. Did you follow your nose?

(Laughter in the galleries)

A. Are you playing games with me?

Q. Answer the question, please.

A. No. I didn't follow my nose.

Q. Could you see her?

A. No.

Q. Hear her?

A. No.

Q. Then how could you possibly know she was there?

A. How did Tom Quillan know? Or Cora Simard? Or poor Vic Mooney? How did any of them know?

Q. Answer the question, miss. This is hardly the place or the time for impertinence.

A. But they did say they 'just knew,' didn't they? I read Mrs Simard's testimony in the paper! And what about the fire hydrants that opened themselves? And the gas pumps that broke their own locks and turned themselves on? The power lines that climbed down off their poles! And—

Q. Miss Snell, please—

A. Those things are in the record of this Commission's proceedings!

Q. This is not an issue here.

A. Then what *is?* Are you looking for the truth or just a scapegoat?

Q. You deny you had prior knowledge of Carrie White's whereabouts?

A. Of course I do. It's an absurd idea.

Q. Oh? And why is it absurd?

A. Well, if you're suggesting some kind of conspiracy, it's absurd because Carrie was dying when I found her. It

207

could not have been an easy way to die.

Q. If you had no prior knowledge of her whereabouts, how could you go directly to her location?

A. Oh, you stupid man! Have you listened to anything that's been said here? Everybody knew it was Carrie! Anyone could have found her if they had put their minds to it.

Q. But not just anyone found her. You did. Can you tell us why people did not show up from all over, like iron filings drawn to a magnet?

A. She was weakening rapidly. I think that perhaps the ... the zone of her influence was shrinking.

Q. I think you will agree that that is a relatively uninformed supposition.

A. Of course it is. On the subject of Carrie White, we're all relatively uninformed.

Q. Have it your way, Miss Snell. Now if we could turn to ...

At first, when she climbed up the enbankment between Henry Drain's meadow and the parking lot of The Cavalier, she thought Carrie was dead. Her figure was halfway across the parking lot, and she looked oddly shrunken and crumpled. Sue was reminded of dead animals she had seen on 495—woodchucks, groundhogs, skunks—that had been crushed by speeding trucks and station wagons.

But the presence was still in her mind, vibrating stubbornly, repeating the call letters of Carrie White's personality over and over. An essence of Carrie, a *gestalt*. Muted now, not strident, not announcing itself with a clarion, but waxing and waning in steady oscillations.

Unconscious.

Sue climbed over the guard rail that bordered the parking lot, feeling the heat of the fire against her face.

208

The Cavalier was a wooden frame building, and it was burning briskly. The charred remains of a car were limned in flame to the right of the back door. Carrie had done that. She did not go to look and see if anyone had been in it. It didn't matter, not now.

She walked over to where Carrie lay on her side, unable to hear her own footsteps under the hungry crackle of the fire. She looked down at the curled-up figure with a bemused and bitter pity. The knife hilt protruded cruelly from her shoulder, and she was lying in a small pool of blood—some of it was trickling from her mouth. She looked as if she had been trying to turn herself over when unconsciousness had taken her. Able to start fires, pull down electric cables, able to kill almost by thought alone; lying here unable to turn herself over.

Sue knelt, took her by one arm and the unhurt shoulder, and gently turned her on to her back.

Carrie moaned thickly, and her eyes fluttered. The perception of her in Sue's mind sharpened, as if a mental picture was coming into focus.

(who's there)

And Sue, without thought, spoke in the same fashion:
(me sue snell)

Only there was no need to think of her name. The thought of herself as herself was neither words nor pictures. The realization suddenly brought everything up close, made it real, and compassion for Carrie broke through the dullness of her shock.

And Carrie with faraway, dumb reproach:
(you tricked me you all tricked me)
(carrie i don't even know what happened is tommy)
(you tricked me that happened trick trick trick o dirty trick)

The mixture of image and emotion was staggering, indescribable. Blood. Sadness. Fear. The latest dirty trick in a long series of dirty tricks: they flashed by in a dizzying shuffle that made Sue's mind reel helplessly, hopelessly. They shared the awful totality of perfect knowledge.

(carrie don't don't don't hurts me)

Now girls throwing sanitary napkins, chanting, laughing, Sue's face mirrored in her own mind: ugly, caricatured all mouth, cruelly beautiful.

(see the dirty tricks see my whole life one long dirty trick)

(look carrie look inside me)

And Carrie looked.

The sensation was terrifying. Her mind and nervous system had become a library. Someone in desperate need ran through her, fingers trailing lightly over shelves of books, lifting some out, scanning them, putting them back, letting some fall, leaving the pages to flutter wildly

(glimpses that's me as a kid hate him daddy o mommy wide lips o teeth bobby pushed me o my knee car want to ride in the car we're going to see aunt cecily mommy come quick i made pee)

in the wind of memory; and still on and on, finally reaching a shelf marked TOMMY, subheaded PROM. Books thrown open, flashes of experience, marginal notations in all the hieroglyphs of emotion, more complex than the Rosetta Stone.

Looking. Finding more than Sue herself had suspected—love for Tommy, jealousy, selfishness, a need to subjugate him to her will on the matter of taking Carrie, disgust for Carrie herself,

(she could take better care of herself she does look just like a GODDAM TOAD)

hate for Miss Desjardin, hate for herself.

But no ill will for Carrie personally, no plan to get her in front of everyone and undo her.

The feverish feeling of being raped in her most secret

corridors began to fade. She felt Carrie pulling back, weak and exhausted.

(why didn't you just leave me alone)

(carrie i)

(momma would be alive i killed my momma i want her o it hurts my chest my shoulder o o o i want my momma)

(carrie i)

And there was no way to finish that thought, nothing there to complete it with. Sue was suddenly overwhelmed with terror, the worse because she could put no name to it: The bleeding freak on this oil-stained asphalt suddenly seemed meaningless and awful in its pain and dying.

(o momma i'm scared momma *MOMMA*)

Sue tried to pull away, to disengage her mind, to allow Carrie at least the privacy of her dying, and was unable to. She felt that she was dying herself and did not want to see this preview of her own eventual end.

(carrie let me GO)

(Momma Momma Momma *oooooooooooo OOOOOOO*)

The mental scream reached a flaring, unbelievable crescendo and then suddenly faded. For a moment Sue felt as if she were watching a candle flame disappear down a long, black tunnel at a tremendous speed.

(she's dying o my god i'm feeling her die)

And then the light was gone, and the last conscious thought had been

(momma i'm sorry where)

and it broke up and Sue was tuned in only on the blank, idiot frequency of the physical nerve endings that would take hours to die.

She stumbled away from it, holding her arms out in front of her like a blind woman, toward the edge of the parking lot. She tripped over the knee-high guard rail and tumbled down the embankment. She got to her feet and

211

stumbled into the field, which was filling with mystic white pockets of ground mist. Crickets chirruped mindlessly and a whippoorwill

(whippoorwill somebody's dying)

called in the great stillness of morning.

She began to run, breathing deep in her chest, running from Tommy, from the fires and explosions, from Carrie, but mostly from the final horror—that last lighted thought carried swiftly down into the black tunnel of eternity, followed by the blank, idiot hum of prosaic electricity.

The after-image began to fade reluctantly, leaving a blessed, cooling darkness in her mind that knew nothing. She slowed, halted, and became aware that something had begun to happen. She stood in the middle of the great and misty field, waiting for realization.

Her rapid breathing slowed, slowed, caught suddenly as if on a thorn—

And suddenly vented itself in one howling, cheated scream.

As she felt the slow course of dark menstrual blood down her thighs.

Part Three

Wreckage

ANDOVER MERCY HOSPITAL/REPORT OF DECEASE

Name <u>White   Carietta   N.</u>   by_____
      (Last)   (First)   (Middle)

Address <u>47 Carlin Street</u>

       <u>Chamberlain, Maine 02249</u>

Emergency Room <u>None</u>   Ambulance <u>#16</u>

Treatment administered <u>None</u>   D.O.A. <u>X</u>
                                              YES NO

Time of Death <u>May 28, 1979 - 2:00 AM (approx.)</u>

Cause of Death <u>Hemorrhage, shock, coronary occlusion</u>

<u>and/or coronary thrombosis (possible)</u>

Person identifying deceased <u>Susan D. Snell</u>

                 <u>19 Back Chamberlain Road</u>

                 <u>Chamberlain, Maine 02249</u>

Next of kin <u>None</u>

Body to be released to <u>Commonwealth of Maine</u>

Doctor in attendance_____

Pathologist_____

From the national AP ticker, Friday, June 5, 1979:

CHAMBERLAIN, MAINE (AP)

STATE OFFICIALS SAY THAT THE DEATH TOLL IN
CHAMBERLAIN STANDS AT 409, WITH 49 STILL LISTED
AS MISSING. INVESTIGATION CONCERNING CARIETTA
WHITE AND THE SO-CALLED 'TK' PHENOMENA
CONTINUES AMID PERSISTENT RUMOURS THAT AN
AUTOPSY ON THE WHITE GIRL HAS UNCOVERED CERTAIN
UNUSUAL FORMATIONS IN THE CEREBRUM AND
CEREBELLUM OF THE BRAIN. THIS STATE'S GOVERNOR
HAS APPOINTED A BLUE-RIBBON COMMITTEE TO STUDY
THE ENTIRE TRAGEDY. ENDS. FINAL JUNE 5 030 N AP

From *The Lewiston Daily Sun*, Sunday, September 7
(p. 3):

The Legacy of TK:
Scorched Earth and Scorched Hearts

CHAMBERLAIN—Prom Night is history now. Pundits
have been saying for centuries that time heals all wounds,
but the hurt of this small Western Maine town may be
mortal. The residential streets are still there on the town's
East Side, guarded by graceful Oaks that have stood for
two hundred years, the trim saltboxes and ranch styles on
Morin Street and Brickyard Hill are still neat and
undamaged. But this New England pastoral lies on the
rim of a blackened and shattered hub, and many of the
neat houses have FOR SALE signs on their front lawns.
Those still occupied are marked by black wreaths on front
doors. Bright-yellow Allied vans and orange U-Hauls of
varying sizes are a common sight on Chamberlain's
streets these days.

The town's major industry, Chamberlain Mills and
Weaving, still stands, untouched by the fire that raged

over much of the town on those two days in May. But it has only been running one shift since July 4th, and according to mill president William A. Chamblis, further lay-offs are a strong possibility. 'We have the orders,' Chamblis said, 'but you can't run a mill without people to punch the time clock. We don't have them. I've gotten notice from thirty-four men since August 15th. The only thing we can see to do now is close up the dye house and job our work out. We'd hate to let the men go, but this thing is getting down to a matter of financial survival.'

Roger Fearon has lived in Chamberlain for twenty-two years, and has been with the mill for eighteen of those years. He has risen during that time from a third-floor bagger making seventy-three cents an hour to dye-house foreman; yet he seems strangely unmoved by the possibility of losing his job. 'I'd lose a damned good wage,' Fearon said. 'It's not something you take lightly. The wife and I have talked it over. We could sell the house—it's worth $20,000 easy—and although we probably won't realize half of that, we'll probably go ahead and put it up. Doesn't matter. We don't really want to live in Chamberlain any more. Call it what you want, but Chamberlain has gone bad for us.'

Fearon is not alone. Henry Kelly, proprietor of a tobacco shop and soda fountain called the Kelly Fruit until Prom Night levelled it, has no plans to rebuild. 'The kids are gone,' he shrugs. 'If I opened up again, there'd be too many ghosts in too many corners. I'm going to take the insurance money and retire to St Petersburg.'

A week after the tornado of '54 had cut its path of death and destruction through Worcester, the air was filled with the sound of hammers, the smell of new timber, and a feeling of optimism and human resilience. There is none of that in Chamberlain this fall. The main road has

217

been cleared of rubble and that is about the extent of it. The faces that you meet are full of dull hopelessness. Men drink beer without talking in Frank's Bar on the corner of Sullivan Street, and women exchange tales of grief and loss in back yards. Chamberlain has been declared a disaster area, and money is available to help put the town back on its feet and begin rebuilding the business district.

But the main business of Chamberlain in the last four months has been funerals.

Four hundred and forty are now known dead, eighteen more still unaccounted for. And sixty-seven of the dead were Ewen High School Seniors on the verge of graduation. It is this, perhaps, more than anything else, that has taken the guts out of Chamberlain.

They were buried on June 1 and 2 in three mass ceremonies. A memorial service was held on June 3 in the town square. It was the most moving ceremony that this reporter has ever witnessed. Attendance was in the thousands, and the entire assemblage was still as the school band, stripped from fifty-six to a bare forty, played the school song and taps.

There was a sombre graduation ceremony the following week at neighbouring Motton Academy, but there were only fifty-two Seniors left to graduate. The valedictorian, Henry Stampel, broke into tears halfway through his speech and could not continue. There were no Graduation Night parties following the ceremony; the Seniors merely took their diplomas and went home.

And still, as the summer progressed, the hearses continued to roll as more bodies were discovered. To some residents it seemed that each day the scab was ripped off again, so that the wound could bleed afresh.

If you are one of the many curiosity-seekers who have been through Chamberlain in the last week, you have seen

218

a town that may be suffering from terminal cancer of the spirit. A few people, looking lost, wander through the aisles of the A&P. The Congregational Church on Carlin Street is gone, swept away by fire, but the brick Catholic Church still stands on Elm Street, and the trim Methodist Church on outer Main Street, although singed by fire, is unhurt. Yet attendance has been poor. The old men still sit on the benches in Courthouse Square, but there is little interest in the checkerboards or even in conversation.

The over-all impression is one of a town that is waiting to die. It is not enough, these days, to say that Chamberlain will never be the same. It may be closer to the truth to say that Chamberlain will simply never again be.

Excerpt from a letter dated June ninth from Principal Henry Grayle to Peter Philpott, Superintendent of Schools:

. . . and so I feel I can no longer continue in my present position, feeling, as I do, that such a tragedy might have been averted if I had only had more foresight. I would like you to accept my resignation effective as of July 1, if this is agreeable to you and your staff . . .

Excerpt from a letter dated June eleventh from Rita Desjardin, instructor of Physical Education, to Principal Henry Grayle:

. . . am returning my contract to you at this time. I feel that I would kill myself before ever teaching again. Late at night I keep thinking: If I had only reached out to that girl, if only, if only . . .

Found painted on the lawn of the house lot where the

219

White bungalow had been located:

CARRIE WHITE IS BURNING FOR HER SINS
JESUS NEVER FAILS

From 'Telekinesis: Analysis and Aftermath' (*Science Yearbook*, 1981), by Dean D. L. McGuffin:

In conclusion, I would like to point out the grave risk authorities are taking by burying the Carrie White affair under the bureaucratic mat—and I am speaking specifically of the so-called White Commission. The desire among politicians to regard TK as a once-in-a-lifetime phenomenon seems very strong, and while this may be understandable it is not acceptable. The possibility of a recurrence, genetically speaking, is 99 per cent. It's time we planned now for what may be . . .

From *Slang Terms Explained: A Parents' Guide*, by John R. Coombs (New York: The Lighthouse Press, 1985), p. 73:

to rip off a Carrie: To cause either violence or destruction; mayhem, confusion; (2) to commit arson (from Carrie White, 1963-1979)

From *The Shadow Exploded* (p. 201):

Elsewhere in this book mention is made of a page in one of Carrie White's school notebooks where a line from a famous rock poet of the '60s, Bob Dylan, was written repeatedly, as if in desperation.

It might not be amiss to close this book with a few lines from another Bob Dylan song, lines that might serve as Carrie's epitaph: *I wish I could write you a melody so*

*plain/That would save you, dear lady, from going insane/
That would ease you and cool you and cease the pain/Of
your useless and pointless knowledge . . .*

From *My Name Is Susan Snell* (p. 98):

This little book is done now. I hope it sells well so I can go
someplace where nobody knows me. I want to think
things over, decide what I'm going to do between now and
the time when my light is carried down that long tunnel
into blackness . . .

From the conclusion of The State Investigatory Board of
Maine in connection with the events of May 27-28 in
Chamberlain, Maine:

. . . and so we must conclude that, while an autopsy
performed on the subject indicates some cellular changes
which *may* indicate the presence of *some* paranormal
power, we find no reason to believe that a recurrence is
possible or even likely . . .

Excerpt from a letter dated May 3, 1988, from Amelia
Jenks, Royal Knob, Tennessee, to Sandra Jens, Maiken,
Georgia:

. . . and your little neece is growin like a weed, awfull big
for only 2. She has blue eyes like her daddy and my blond
hair but that will porubly go dark. Still she is awfull pretty
& I think sometimes when she is asleep how she looks like
our momma.

The other day wile she was playin in the dirt beside the
house I sneeked around and saw the funnyest thing.
Annie was playin with her brothers marbles only they was
mooving around all by themselfs. Annie was giggeling

221

and laffing but I was a little skared. Some of them marbles was going right up & down. It reminded me of gramma, do you remember when the law came up that time after Pete and there guns flew out of there hands and grammie just laffed and laffed. And she use to be able to make her rocker go even when she wasen in it. I gave me a reel bad turn to think on it. I shure hope she don't get heartspels like grammie did, remember?

Well I must go & do a wash so give my best to Rich and take care to send us some pitchers when you can. Still our Annie is awfull pretty & her eyes are as brite as buttons. I bet she'll be a worldbeeter someday.

All my love,

Melia